THE GRAND DAYS OF TRAVEL

THE GRAND DAYS OF TRAVEL

Charles Owen

Windward/Webb & Bower

A *Webb&Bower* Book
Edited, designed and produced by
Webb & Bower (Publishers) Limited, Exeter, England.

Copyright © 1979 Webb & Bower (Publishers) Ltd
Text copyright © 1979 Charles Owen

'Windward' an imprint owned by W H Smith & Sons Ltd

Registered Number 237811 England.
Trading as: WHS Distributors, Euston
Street, Freemen's Common, Aylestone
Road, Leicester, LE2 7SS.

ISBN 07112 0006 8

Designed by Vic Giolitto
Picture Research by Anne Horton

Typeset by Keyspools Ltd, Golborne, Lancs
Printed and bound in Great Britain by
Butler and Tanner Ltd, Frome

CONTENTS

PREFACE

Most people who move about the world today, from one airport to the next, if not businessmen or contract workers in bored or bemused transit, are tourists on package holidays. A characteristic of the package tour is the protection of a herd of customers from reality. Wherever they go, in bus, airport lounge, aircraft, hotel or restaurant, the environment is stereotyped, synthetic and predictable: temperatures, piped music, table d'hôte food, décor and basic amenities are much the same everywhere. The scene and the scenery are viewed passively through glass: through the windows of vehicles, lodgings and places of entertainment. And, when their packaged day ends, the chances are that the visitors, retiring to their rooms, will continue peering lazily at life through the screen of a TV set.

Half a century ago, well within living memory, international travel, catering overtly for the relatively rich, rare and energetic, was hardly at all like this. Generally, tracks were beaten and paths smooth but the unexpected often happened and, because the speed of advance was not very fast and every scene differed vividly from the last, there was a sense of adventure and discovery in most journeys. Service adapted itself with alacrity to a customer's tastes and foibles and, being largely paid for after the event, could be costly to the provider if it did not please. In particular, the tip was a reward for service well given rather than a levy made in advance, regardless of results.

The most notable hallmark of that period of travel was the adoption universally, at the higher-priced levels of public transportation, of a more or less 'Grand Hotel' ambience in a variety of forms. The great ocean liners, with their vast pillared lounges and club-like 'flunkey' service, each ship with its own distinctive character, provided a setting for the great figures travelling from one capital city or fashionable resort to another. While statesmen, bankers, newspaper tycoons and film stars plied their gracious way across the Atlantic, the rulers and managers of the world and their consorts sailed the stately routes from Europe to the colonies and dominions over which they held sway. Although urgent messages could be exchanged by radio, the world, for the most part, was shut out during the six Atlantic days or the several weeks en route to the Orient: thus both the journey and the arrival were major events.

Politics, business and pleasure depended largely on the movement of these ships or, for shorter distances, of the international express train. The latter, particularly the elegant Pullman and Wagon-lits coaches, was a microcosm of the sumptuous Ritz Hotel manner. While liner passengers trailed their foamy wakes across the oceans, train travellers would be lurching their clacketty way from New York to San Francisco, Ostend to Berlin, Calais to Rome, Bombay to Calcutta, Peking to Shanghai, Cape Town to Johannesburg, Buenos Aires to Santiago. A wealthy family with retinue on a one-thousand-mile journey across Europe from, say, Northern Italy to London, might expect to spend two days on the trip. The first lap of the journey, giving a midday arrival in Paris,

Opposite: The French liner *Normandie* leaves Le Havre for New York in 1935, in the era when the great ocean liners provided a setting for the famous figures travelling the world.

6

would have been by sleeping car; a heavy dinner in the restaurant car would have been shaken down already on the way. In the afternoon, there would have been fresh air and sightseeing in the city for the women and children, leaving father free to keep a business appointment or two. Overnight respite would have been taken in a Paris hotel, conveyance of passengers and baggage from the station having employed two or three porters and a pair of taxis. Thence, next day, the passengers would have travelled to England by *Golden Arrow* Pullman and its special connecting cross-Channel ship, with banquet-style lunch held down, with luck, across the Straits of Dover. On landing in Kent, a night in a lavish palm-courted hotel was followed next morning by the last lap to Victoria.

Two other forms of travel, now commonplace, were then in their ebullient adolescence, the preserve mainly of the most wealthy, the most adventurous or the most eccentric: touring by motor car and transit by aeroplane. Of course, there was a growing network of motor buses and charabancs in the more developed countries but, as yet, these were largely for the common people. For the few, the appropriate vehicle by road would have been a high-backed limousine or an open touring car with its flimsy, collapsible hood, raised only to keep the rain out.

Air travel, apart from the relatively popular short-haul routes in North America, was another experience to be enjoyed only by the very few. Here, once again, the trappings of land travel were repeated: day flights by flying boat, including Grand Hotel catering in miniature, with passengers on cushioned cane chairs at a lightweight table, followed by overnight stops at first-class hotels near the landing stages. Thus, for example, in the mid-1930s, the intrepid traveller could make his way from London to Hong Kong in ten days by a once-weekly (and commendably reliable) Imperial Airways service.

This book is about those heydays of travel, in particular about the inter-war period 1919–39. Concerned with travel by ship, train, car and aeroplane, it aims to recapture some of the style and flavour, the ambience and the environment of wealthy travellers and those who served them on stations, quays and aerodromes; in hotels and restaurants; on board ocean liners, trains and aeroplanes; in motor cars, rickshaws and taxi cabs. Some of our readers were there and may enjoy being reminded of those 'grander' days; some, travelling backwards in time, may share the pleasures vicariously; others, with a thirst for history, may find that it repays study. But whatever the individual reasons we hope that it will provide interest and entertainment to all.

CHARLES OWEN Spring 1979

1 RETROSPECT 1919

In 1919, the carnage and disruption of the First World War ended, a new era of international travel in the Grand Hotel manner was at hand. The affluent middle classes, their ranks swollen by the growing band of professional men, managers and ex-officers, were ready for a spree.

Now, many members of the new élite, with limited time for holidays, chose to buy enjoyment in the summer when the weather was good, rather than in winter, the time preferred hitherto by the idler rich for their forays overseas. Faced with a new demand for glamour and sophistication, speed and mobility, in preference to leisurely and over-grandiose opulence, the purveyors of travel, particularly of rail and, later, air services, were able with the greater standardization of basic amenity in an expanding market to keep charges down and, in good years, profits up.

In France there survived as a poignant reminder of holocaust numerous wooden railway vans bearing the crisp warning '40 *hommes 8 chevaux*', this being the cargo authorized in war by the military authorities. An interesting scale of values: was the tare fixed to enable the horses to lie down while the men stood; or was there segregation of the species? Of course, people were used to segregation, if only among themselves: white did not fraternize with black, bowler hat with cloth cap, un-chaperoned high-school virgin with common man. As it happened, common men, black or white, did not travel much or very far, unless as migrants, pilgrims or soldiers; and then they were safely out of the way in steerage, third or *camion* class. The age of plush packaged travel for the masses lay at least a generation ahead.

Thus, there was little except fleeting glimpses of the passing scene, viewed in company with kindred spirits, to disturb the comfortable reveries of the wealthy traveller, cosily secure in his well cushioned and carpeted accommodation. On land or overland in most countries at this time the sturdy train provided the normal mode of transit, and a plethora of railway companies vied for his favour. Their networks, shown as a web of black lines, dominated the maps of most advanced countries; roads were hardly featured and air routes not at all.

All this competition was to lead between the world wars to great advances in travel speeds, convenience and creature comforts, a natural outcome after many years of the pioneering work of two notable figures in railway history: the American, George Pullman, and the Belgian, Georges Nagelmackers. It was the former who, in the 1860s, introduced purpose-built sleeping cars, his early types being convertible by day into saloons or dining-rooms; and in later years the Pullman day-car spread from America into several European railway systems. With the advent of further refinements, equivalent to those provided in hotels and steam ships, the way was clear for the introduction in the second half of the nineteenth century of rail journeys of several days' duration.

But suitable trains were slow to evolve due to two obstacles: the parochialism of rail operators in adjoining countries who were reluctant to accept on their lines rolling

Interior View of the New Pullman Palace Sleeping Cars now Running on the Northern Pacific R. R. through between St. Paul and Portland.
(See inside page for more about these Cars, rates, etc.)

Luxury cross-country travel by train began in America in the 1860s with George Pullman's sleeping cars, convertible by day into lounges. The interior of a 'Palace' car of 1876 is shown in its daytime guise (left). (Below) illustrates a lower but still tolerable level of amenity.

stock belonging to their neighbours; and the difficulty of coupling together and hauling trains which, in such vital respects as braking systems, buffer alignments and overall dimensions, were far from standardized. It fell to Nagelmackers to find an acceptable formula and the financial backing to give it effect.

The company which he formed became, perhaps, the most famous name in railway history: *Compagnie Internationale des Wagons-lits et des Grands Express Européens*. Looking back, his idea seems simple enough: he designed and provided carriages equipped, furnished and staffed for his passengers' needs. He delegated haulage and operation to the railway managements in the countries

An *Orient Express* menu.

through which his trains were to travel, while the local managements were paid for their function partly from a share of the proceeds of tickets sold to long-distance passengers through Nagelmackers' agencies and partly from income derived from mail-carrying contracts.

The first of the new-style international expresses, the world-famous *Orient Express*, made its inaugural run in 1883, bringing Constantinople to within eighty hours of Paris; and the journey included legs by local steamer and train beyond Bucharest which, initially, was the train's destination. According to de Blowitz, foreign correspondent of *The Times*, the train was 'a marvellous sight' comprising 'two sleeping cars, two vans for baggage and provisions, and a restaurant car'. Twelve customers at a time could be accommodated in the warm, gas-lit restaurant to enjoy an *haute cuisine* menu brought to them by immaculate stewards swaying to and fro between the cramped, coal-fired galley and the smart, white-linened tables.

Almost as old as the *Orient Express*, although it began its life under a different name, was the all-sleeping car Paris–Mediterranean express, the *Blue Train*; for many years this train, among others, provided through-coaches from Calais for a 'mixed cargo of English aristocrats, merchants' wives with marriageable daughters and well-heeled gamblers'. From Hook of Holland, Ostend and Boulogne other important expresses also collected their loads from the connecting packets.

Among the most romantic were those 'special' trains which conveyed the imperial rulers across the European land mass to Mediterranean ports, whence they could be taken on by sea through the Suez Canal to India and beyond. A forerunner of these trains, the *Malle des Indes*, began life as long ago as 1855, carrying British mails to Marseilles to be loaded there into P & O ships, so saving several days in transit.

Another influence was that of fashionable holiday areas. The most notable, perhaps, was the Côte d'Azur which, to a large extent, had Queen Victoria to thank for its evolution for, in the wake of royalty 'there inevitably came the gentry and the nouveaux riches, the international smart sets and the social climbers with their trunks and fine clothes, servants, hat-boxes, jewel cases and bulging money-bags'. From the turn of the century direct expresses were bringing to this coast wealthy nationals from St Petersburg, Berlin, Amsterdam, Brussels, Vienna and Rome, and 'the arrival of *trains de luxe* in the Riviera from all major capitals of Europe transformed the area in a few years into a rip-roaring pleasure resort'.

Meanwhile, the Americans were taking their own important steps forward in the railway sphere. The United States opened its first cross-country route in 1869 and, within twenty years there were four such routes in the United States and one in Canada. Sumptuous parlour cars were now the order of the day; and, for a time, private ownership of a luxury railway carriage was a status symbol almost as desirable as the ownership of a smart yacht. The most elegant of these private cars, referred to as 'mansions

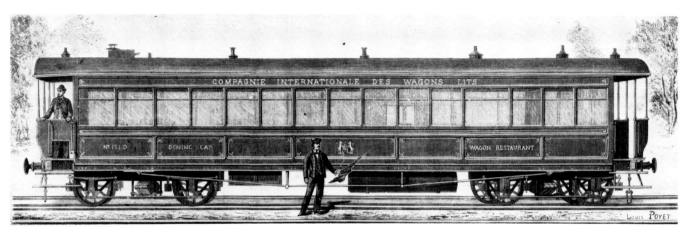

In Europe Georges Nagelmackers'
Orient Express opened the way to
international long-distance
journeys in style and comfort.
(Below) shows this pioneering
train under way. Besides its two
sleeping cars, there was a dining
car (below).

on rails', were nearly a hundred feet long and cost their owners up to $$\frac{1}{2}$$ million to acquire, the embellishments sometimes including open grates, printing presses, wine coolers, fine woods and glassware, servants and milk-producing cattle.

When it came to naming trains, no one was more imaginative than the Americans, at least seven hundred such trains having been introduced over the years. Some of these reached standards of comfort superior to those obtainable in other countries. The New York–Boston express seventy years ago offered private state-rooms, observation cars furnished as club sitting-rooms, two dining cars and a travelling staff of maids and porters; and names such as the *Twentieth Century Limited* and the *Broadway Limited* on the New York–Chicago run were to become world-famous.

At the opening of the twentieth century, the golden age of railways was near its peak. At the main destinations, often adjoining the station, large and splendid hotels under railway management awaited the traveller's pleasure. Where a rail journey involved a cross-channel passage, connecting packets were provided, also under railway management, to ply between specially designed transit ports. Similar facilities, albeit larger, were provided also at ocean-liner terminals, ensuring that the ship-borne traveller could start and finish his journey in the manner to which the ship owners made him feel accustomed. For at sea, as on land, and particularly in the North Atlantic, the race for the rich man's patronage was on.

Whereas the train is an expression of the industrial age, the ship is as old as history. In the steam age, however, thanks to the inventive brilliance of engineers, both were able to evolve into fast, reliable and truly elegant forms, the core of the growth of worldwide communications. Nevertheless, while the train held sway on land, the navy-protected ocean liner became the true, global sinew of both commerce and empire; and, in performing this function, it provided a setting in which leaders of government, industry, the arts and fashion could demonstrate their wealth and power, their stylish way of life and their serene self-satisfaction.

The story of Cunard is at the heart of the story of the ocean liner in its heyday; and the prolonged competition between shipping companies of several countries to become holder of the transatlantic speed record, the Blue Riband, is at the heart of the Cunard story. The first pace-setter was Cunard's tiny wooden paddle-steamer *Britannia*, which averaged 10.56 knots on the Halifax–Liverpool leg of its maiden voyage homeward in 1840. Ten years later, with the American Collins Line's bid for the Blue Riband, the international battle began in earnest. The next major contender was the British White Star Line, to be amalgamated later with Cunard. Several other shipowners were now in the field but, over the years, Cunard became the foremost champion.

The most famous Blue Riband holder in this century was undoubtedly Cunard's *Mauretania*, which managed the incredible feat of being the fastest liner on the run from

1907 right through to 1929, and of improving its record-breaking average speeds in that time from 22.21 to 27.22 knots. German, Italian and French ships then had their turns as winners until *Queen Mary* recovered the trophy for Cunard in 1938, holding it right through to 1952, when America's *United States* claimed it finally, with a sensational sprint eastbound averaging 35.59 knots. Cunard's superb *QE2*, lone *grande ligne* survivor on the transatlantic run, would win a beauty contest but the Blue Riband, the prize for speed, stays firmly in America.

The other part of the ocean-liner story, less loudly trumpeted, lay along the imperial routes, mainly those connecting Europe with its dominions and colonies across the seas. Here again, many shipping lines competed for a lucrative traffic provided largely at the expense of governments or large corporations, comprising soldiers and civil servants, administrators and engineers, planters and salesmen. The best known of these routes passed through the Suez Canal, one fine, dignified ship after

As this 1892 photograph of Cunard's *Campania* shows, the shape and style, if not the size and speed, of the great twentieth-century liners were already discernible by the late nineteenth century.

The opening of the Suez Canal in 1869, by shortening dramatically the eastward shipping routes, transformed the means of trade and communication between Europe and many of its overseas possessions.

another sailing in stately procession. The leading name on ships travelling to India, the Far East and Australia was the British P & O Company, 'in its own view the lifeline of what the sun was said never to set upon, relating closely to the Establishment, holding a special place among the leading Navies of the world – these evidently being in order of importance first, the Royal Navy; second, the P & O; third, the British Merchant Navy in general.' P & O passenger ships still ply the seas today but mainly on pleasure cruises and not as Somerset Maugham, among other reporters, would have us remember them.

But the grand old days of travel, the last two decades of which form the theme of this book, were numbered. The airliner, soon to supersede the ocean liner and the long-distance international express train, came slowly but noisily into prominence from 1919, due partly to a surfeit of unemployed military aviators and an availability of aircraft converted from wartime bombing types. Here was a great new travel opportunity, presenting new scope for adventure and excitement and new prospects for invention and investment.

In 1919, only ten years after Blériot became the first person to fly the English Channel, the Atlantic was crossed several times by air. In May, an American Curtiss NC4 flying boat flew from New York to Plymouth, with a stop en route in the Azores. In June came the first ever non-stop transatlantic flight by aeroplane: this time it was a British feat, the means being a converted Vickers Vimy bomber and the trajectory Newfoundland to Ireland. Then in July the British rigid airship R34 made the first Atlantic crossing by a 'lighter-than-air' vehicle.

Above: Foretaste of first-class standards of comfort, a commonplace of modern airliners: the interior of a 'passenger aeroplane' in 1919. The luxurious ambience depicted by this artist was not, however, typical.

Right: For some years airships held sway over the long-distance transocean air routes. This British pioneer flew the Atlantic in 1919, one month after the first non-stop crossing by aeroplane.

Meanwhile, in Europe, it had become the practice for VIPs, including Lloyd George and Winston Churchill, to be flown in Royal Air Force aircraft from London to Paris to attend the peace talks at Versailles. Then, in February 1919, the first sustained daily passenger air service opened in Germany with a Berlin–Leipzig–Weimar service, whilst in the same month France laid claim to the first international passenger flight with conveyance of a plane-load of eleven passengers from Paris to London. However, the honour of starting the first-ever *scheduled* international passenger service went to Britain's Air Transport and Travel with its flight by a De Havilland 16 from Hounslow to Le Bourget. Within a month two other British companies were also running cross-Channel services.

1919 also saw the first regular airship service, another German record, this being between Friedrichshafen and Berlin; Holland became host country to the newly formed International Air Traffic Association; and the first airmail services were introduced: one from Folkestone to Cologne, serving army units in the Rhineland, and the other connecting Chicago with Cleveland. During the next twenty years, while the Atlantic would remain beyond the endurance of non-stop heavier-than-air machines, the world at large would become criss-crossed by air services, dominated on the intercontinental routes for a short, hopeful period by the airship and then, more securely, by the flying boat. However, it would need the advent of the Second World War and jet propulsion to shrink the size of the world before it could be laid at the airline operators' feet.

But the main and most significant inter-war upset in the realms of travel was the motor car, key through individual mobility to new wide-ranging boundaries of family, social, recreational and business life. The car was already well in evidence before the First World War, the modern car, according to one authority, having originated in 1891 with the advent of the front-engined Panhard; and by 1904 several hundred firms all over the world were making cars of a kind. In the following decade came the 8-cylinder car and, most significantly, Henry Ford's mass-produced Model T which 'could go wherever there was a road', and frequently where there was none. It was a masterpiece of mechanical simplicity, it was easy to operate, and it could be repaired by anyone with an elementary knowledge of machinery.

In 1919, clearly, the motor car was poised to become an

essential vehicle for the wealthy to drive themselves on the highway, to race in or to ride in loftily with uniformed chauffeurs at the wheel. However, despite the Ford augury, no one at the time could foresee how the car would eventually become the hobby, extension of the home and substitute for muscle power for people of every class in every advanced country in the world: and, alas, in the process dominate and, to an extent, pollute the environment while helping to squander the world's energy resources.

Perhaps it is as well that in transportation matters, as in other human affairs, foresight has always been limited since, otherwise, the story of the aeroplane and the car, and to a lesser extent of their predecessors, the steam ship and the train, would have been even more marked by greed and self-indulgence, and the consequences would have been even more devastating.

1919: *our* story opens here. Its concern is with the joys of travel, with romance and grandeur, luxury and service, enjoyment and achievement in motion; esoteric values, conscience and philosophy are mentioned only in passing. We start in New York, eagerly, with an ocean voyage in prospect: we begin by going to sea.

The motor car, although at first a status symbol only for the wealthy, was already well in evidence before the First World War. The squire and his carefully dressed wife (above) set off to visit friends one fine day in 1910, while a holiday party (left) takes a short-cut from a landing at Venice Lido.

2 OCEAN TRAVEL: THE NORTH ATLANTIC

Nowhere in New York City is far from the tang and the sound of the ocean. Until a few years ago, from many vantage points on Manhattan Island, anyone looking westward along the straight cross-town streets, could glimpse it, too; could see, looming against the distant sky beyond the Hudson river the soaring shapes of the great ocean liners. On peak sailing days, each at its own pier, the liners lay in serried rows, their noses nuzzling the shoreline like thirsty mammals at the teats of some vastly plentiful udder.

New York was long unique among large cities in receiving in its midst a galaxy of brilliantly diverse vessels linking it directly with the world at large.

Intending passengers high up in their nearby hotels, their labelled baggage assembled in the foyer, passports, steamer tickets and state-room reservations in hand, would listen for the warning siren; on hearing it or on spotting the tell-tale wisp of steam, they would summon the bellhop and, gathering their belongings into a taxi, depart. Within a few minutes they would be on the pier, in the maw of the embarkation process beside the giant side of the waiting liner, part of a scene of orderly confusion: band playing, officials, porters and stewards all around, keyed up with that mixture of dread and exhilaration, of sadness and excitement which, over the centuries, has been the special accompaniment of a ship's sailing for distant lands.

New York was long unique among large cities in receiving in its midst a galaxy of brilliantly diverse vessels linking it directly with the world at large and, predominantly, with the maritime countries of Europe, birthplaces of most New Yorkers' forebears. Even half a generation ago, well into the age of flight, the coming and going of these great ships was still virtually a daily event;

Life on the ocean wave in those grander days: four mementoes.

Champagnes

		Bottle. s. d.	Half-Bottle. s. d.
Pommery & Greno			
1.	Nature, 1926	20 0	1921 10 6
Veuve Clicquot, Ponsardin			
2.	Dry, 1926	20 0	10 6
3.	†Brut	16 0	—
Heidsieck & Co.			
4.	Dry Monopole, 1928	20 0	10 6
G. H. Mumm & Co.			
5.	Cordon Rouge, 1923, 1926	20 0	10 6
	Magnum, 1928, 40/-		
6.	†Extra dry	15 0	8 0
Boilinger & Co.			
7.	Extra quality, very dry, 1928	20 0	10 6
8.	Special Cuvée, very dry, non-vintage ..	18 0	9 6
Lanson Père et Fils			
9.	Extra quality, extra dry, 1926, 1928 ..	20 0	10 6
Pol Roger & Co.			
10.	Cuvée Reserve, extra quality, 1926	20 0	1921 10 6
Ayala & Co.			
11.	Extra quality, extra dry, 1926	18 0	9 6
Louis Roederer			
12.	Extra dry, 1926	18 0	1920 1921 9 6
13.	Non-vintage	15 0	8 0
Perrier Jouet & Co.			
14.	Finest extra quality, 1923, 1926	18 0	1919 9 6

† *Champagnes of a lighter body as referred to in the preface.*

Champagnes

		Bottle. s. d.	Half-Bottle. s. d.
Moët & Chandon			
15.	Dry Imperial, 1926	18 0	1921 9 6
16.	†Brut Imperial	15 0	8 0
Charles Heidsieck			
17.	Extra quality, extra dry, 1926	18 0	9 6
18.	Extra quality, extra dry, 1921	—	—
	Imperial pint, 12/6		
19.	†Sec Gout American	14 0	7 6
Ernest Irroy & Co.			
20.	Carte d'Or, 1920, 1926	18 0	9 6
Piper Heidsieck			
21.	Très sec, 1923	18 0	9 6
George Goulet & Co.			
22.	Extra quality, extra dry, 1920, 1926 ..	18 0	9 6
Krug & Co.			
23.	Private Cuvée, extra sec, 1928	18 0	9 6
Delbeck & Co.			
24.	Extra reserve, extra sec, 1920, 1926	17 6	9 0
Henriot			
25.	†Souverain, extra dry, 1926	14 0	—

† *Champagnes of a lighter body as referred to in the preface.*

R.M.S. Aquitania - Cunard Line

:-: DINNER :-:

FRIVOLITE

Grape Fruit Suprême   Honey Dew Melon

Blue Point Oyster Cocktail   Caviar

Jambon Epicure   Terrine de Foie Gras   Thon a l'Antiboise

Smoked Sturgeon   Herring Roes, Ravigote   Lyon Sausage

Primeurs à la Greque   Cèpes Mariné   Sardines de Nantes

Olives de Lucque   Smoked Salmon   Canapé Rillettes

Salted Almonds   Peanuts   Pecans

POTAGE

Consommé Réjane   Bisque of Lobster, Americaine

Green Turtle au Sherry   Velouté Lafayette

Cold Consommé in Cup   St. Germain au Tapioca

FISH

Pompano Sauté—Amandine

Devilled Whitebait   Fillets of Dover Sole—Bonne Femme

Broiled Split Smelts—Colbert

ENTREE

Boneless Squab en Cocotte—Mascotte

Vol-au-Vent à la Reine   Braised Sweetbreads—Financière

Frog Legs—Figaro

Cold—Terrine of Duckling, Rouennaise

Cold—Cornet of York Ham à la Gelée

JOINT AND POULTRY

Roast Philadelphia Capon—Cranberry Sauce

Smoked Ox Tongue—Crécy

Prime Ribs of Beef—Horseradish Sauce

Punch Romaine

DINER SUGGESTION

Honey Dew Melon

Bisque of Lobster, Americaine

Fillets of Sole, Bonne Femme

Roast Capon, Cranberry Sauce
Spinach en Branches
Rissolees Potatoes

Pears Dame Blanche

Passengers on Special Diet are especially invited
to make known their requirements to the
Head Waiter

The Clocks will be Advanced One Hour at Midnight

S

GRILL (TO ORDER)

Guinea Hen—Planked Club Style

Ham Steaks—Cumberland Sauce   Minute Steak—Valoise

Noisette of Lamb—Tourangelle

VEGETABLES

New String Beans   Broccoli Hollandaise
Fried Egg Plant   Celery, Demi-Glace

Potatoes—Boiled, Rissolées, Gaufrette, Croquette

COOKED (TO ORDER)

Snipe   Pigeon   Poussin   Grain   Jumbo Squab
Pheasant   Rouen Duckling   Partridge

SALAD

Romaine   Calavo   Lettuce   Beatrice
Tropical Comfort   Country Club   Fruit
Thousand Island, French, Russian and Roquefort Dressing

SWEET

Soufflé Pudding Coburg   Canton Pudding

Pears Dame Blanche   Savarin aux Fruits

Pecan Nut Sundae   Compôte of Apples

Profiteroles au Chocolat   Petits Fours

ICES

Napolitaine, Coffee, Strawberry

Vanilla Ice Cream—Apricot Sauce

Biscuit Mousse au Café and Praliné

SAVOURIES

Canapé Cadogan   Croûte Aberdeen   Biscuit Suisse

Mushrooms on Toast   Sardines on Horseback

Dessert   Coffee

but half a century ago these departures, more numerous then, being the sole link with continents across the world, were part of the very life-blood of the city.

At that time, as Douglas Phillips-Birt recalls in his book *When Luxury Went to Sea*, the best-known ships were 'period pieces, they were Charlottenburg Palace, the Gothic Chatsworth; they were all the Ritz Hotels thrown in, amazingly established on the sea. Inevitably, they were described as "floating cities" .... There were the Grosvenor Squares, the Faubourgs Saint Germain, and not a little of what caused some people to describe the Berlin of the day as "Parvenupopolis".... Everything in the environment of the first-class passengers sought to deny the existence of the sea.' A bridge of ships? Almost. For in a typical mid-summer week in 1929, on the eve of the Great Depression, there would be ten or more direct sailings for Europe, with passages on offer from several competing shipping companies, mainly British, French, German, Dutch, Italian and American.

But the lion's share of all this traffic had long been enjoyed by Britain's Cunard Line: to have sailed Cunard to Europe was the *cachet* of the well-connected globe-trotter. At that time this company maintained its own weekly services which operated between New York and Southampton, New York and Liverpool, and New York and London, their ships turning around at Piers 90-2 at the end of West 50th Street, a mere five blocks from Broadway. Up to a dozen liners, varying in tonnage from nearly 50,000 to just under 20,000, in service speeds from about 25 knots to 15 knots, with a total capacity of some 30,000 passengers, were needed to maintain these schedules; and the same company served Canada via the St Lawrence river with a further half-dozen vessels. Concurrently, the British White Star and Canadian Pacific Lines, the former to be absorbed by Cunard in 1934, were also operating impressive fleets of ships in the North Atlantic, including White Star's *Majestic*, then the largest ship afloat and one of a pair providing yet another New York–Southampton regular service.

The star of the Cunard fleet, holder of the transatlantic Blue Riband speed record since 1909 when she averaged 26 knots between Cobh and Sandy Hook, was the four-funnelled, coal-burning *Mauretania*, 'the Grand Old Lady of the Atlantic'. This ship's running mates on the express and, socially, most desirable New York–Southampton run were the newer, oil-burning, *Aquitania* and the ex-German *Berengaria*, with four and three funnels respectively. Each ship, in the eyes of the experienced traveller, had its own distinctive style and personality. The preferred *Aquitania* 'had a Caroline smoking room, an Elizabethan grill room, a Louis XIV dining room and a Palladian lounge, while the swimming pool was inspired by Egyptian remains in the British Museum and flanked by fluted columns of dubious origin.'

Franklin D Roosevelt's impressions are on record: 'Every ship has a soul. But the *Mauretania* had one you could talk to. At times she could be wayward and contrary as a thoroughbred. To no other ship belonged that trick of

hers – that thrust and dip and drive into the seas and through them, which would wreck the rails of the Monkey Island with solid sea, or playfully spatter salt water on the Captain's boiled shirt as he took a turn on the bridge before going down to dinner.'

A Cunard statement at that time explained how the *Mauretania* 'holds the passionate allegiance of whole families of America's highest type, who would rather miss Ascot or the first day of grouse-shooting than cross in any other ship afloat, but the *Mauretania*.' On the other hand, 'the *Aquitania*'s passenger lists tend slightly towards Burke and Debrett ... The people who cross in her are people you might meet at an important Thursday to Monday, where blood and achievement both count ... By day, Harris tweeds ... Chanel jerseys ... indolent conversation and energetic sport. By night a sudden increase of tempo ... a blaze of jewels ... the gleam of ivory shoulders ... gowns, rose, gold, green ...'

S N Behrman records that Duveen sailed from New York in the summer of 1921 in the *Aquitania* with his friends H E and Arabella Huntington who occupied the Gainsborough Suite hung with copies of that master's paintings, including 'The Blue Boy'. Duveen told H E that the original which belonged to the Duke of Westminster 'would be the crown of any collection of English pictures' and, as such, its price would probably be about $600,000. H E being interested, Duveen on reaching London called on the Duke at Grosvenor House, finding him 'extremely receptive to the idea of selling "The Blue Boy", and anything else in the place'. Duveen promptly bought 'The Blue Boy', Reynolds' 'Sarah Siddons as the Tragic Muse' and Gainsborough's 'The Cottage Door', the price for the three being 'slightly more than the figure he had mentioned on the *Aquitania* for "The Blue Boy" alone. The moment the deal was set, Duveen ... telephoned Huntington in Paris to tell him the good news. He had acquired "The Blue Boy" and would deliver it for $620,000 – the $20,000 covered the telephone call.'

We have confirmation from John Malcolm Brinnin in his book *The Sway of the Grand Saloon* of the *Aquitania*'s appeal to the discerning: 'When the young Mr. and Mrs. F. Scott Fitzgerald actually got their hands on a hefty sum of money from the first of Scott's novels to win a big audience, their thoughts turned ... to the best available: first class, no less, on the *Aquitania*. "Lustily splashing their dreams in the dark pool of gratification," wrote Zelda, "their fifty thousand dollars bought a cardboard day-nurse for Bonnie, a second-hand Marmon, a Picasso etching, a white satin dress ... a dress as green as fresh wet paint, two white knickerbocker suits exactly alike, a broker's suit and two first class tickets to Europe."' Even the ex-German *Berengaria*, least favoured of the 'Big Three' 'is accustomed to move through the night brighter than the Milky Way ... everything about the *Berengaria* is on the grand, the opulent scale, she is sensational ... her passenger lists are electric with great names'. On one voyage, in fact, the Prince of Wales himself was a passenger.

The *Mauretania* calls at Plymouth in 1925. In its day star of the Cunard fleet, F D Roosevelt considered it a thoroughbred 'with a soul you could talk to'.

The former German liner, now America's *Leviathan* (right foreground), at Southampton in 1925 with Britain's *Olympic* and (left) *Aquitania*, Cunard's favourite at that time with the top social set.

After New York, the world's best known ocean liner terminal was doubtless Southampton, connected to London by special trains running from the dockside to Waterloo station: a typical heyday scene.

The name of the game was etiquette: to travel well, and be seen to travel well, needed a careful study of the social form. According to Emily Post: 'Very fashionable people as a rule travel a great deal, which means that they are known very well to the head steward, who reserves a table. Mr. and Mrs. Gilding, for instance, if they know that friends of theirs are sailing on the same steamer, ask them to sit at their table ... But most people ... sit wherever the head steward puts them. After a meal or two people always speak to those sitting next to them ... On the deluxe steamers, nearly every one dresses for dinner; some actually in ball dresses, which is in the worst possible taste,

required with decorations, which put Americans, unless they were of military background, at a disadvantage in the matter of crosses, ribbons and miniatures.'

But Basil Woon insists: 'The dinner-jacket is as necessary to an ocean traveler as a tailcoat is to a waiter. Without it you may not, except on the first and last nights out, come down to dinner. Without it you will have to sneak out of the smoking-room at eight P.M. Without it you will have no dances and no Great Moments with the young thing in crêpe-marocain on the lee of the starboard ventilator.' While, for the hours on deck, 'the Plus-Four is now considered absolutely the only garment fit to wear for promenading during the day-light hours.'

France's French Line, next in rank after Cunard for fashionable people, was led by the relatively new *Ile de France*, a fine, dashing ship run with 'Gallic panache', known to the *cognoscenti* as 'The Boulevard of the Atlantic'. Among those who preferred this liner were Toscanini, Maurice Chevalier, Pola Negri and Tallulah Bankhead. Ginger Rogers, at a gala in aid of seamen's charities, collected $50 a dance and $100 a kiss. Noël Coward featured the ship in his play *These Foolish Things*. The Cecil B de Milles 'luxuriated in the great ship ... with its gilded main dining-room, its statues by Baudry and Dejean, its sumptuous bas-reliefs and paintings'. Other notable passengers in the *Ile*'s early years included Marlene Dietrich, Gloria Swanson and Constance Bennett; Lily Pons, Grace Moore and Jeanette Macdonald; John D Rockefeller, Bernard Baruch and the Woolworth heiress, Barbara Hutton.

We know from Don Stanford's book *Ile de France* that this great ship's seven-hundred-seat first-class dining-room was adorned 'in three shades of grey marble from the Pyrenees by the architect Pierre Patout, illuminated by one hundred and twelve *motifs* exquisitely moulded in glass by Lalique, and further decorated with paintings by Vouget and Eddy Legrand and by a magnificent illuminated fountain designed by the famed sculptor Navarre. The dining room was reached by one of the most dramatic staircases ever to delight the heart of a lovely lady arrayed in her finest plumage ... other great artists of the era worked together to produce a tiered concourse of smart little shops in the four-storey well of the Grand Foyer, a Parisian pavement café ... an enormous Grand Salon and Salon de Thé each with windows more than fifteen feet high, a two-storey Smoking Room, a sumptuous Salon de Conversation'. The ship had its practical side, too, for there were 'a modern hospital, a barber shop and a beauty parlour, a dry-cleaning shop, a library, a laundry capable of handling over one hundred thousand pieces of linen per voyage – and even a consecrated Roman Catholic chapel, the first ever to go to sea'.

The *Ile* was, indeed, a lady of her times. For 'these were the Roaring Twenties. This was the era of the flapper and the rolled stocking and the Stutz Bearcat and the coonskin coat, and the Charleston and the Black Bottom and the hip flask.'

But then came the Wall Street crash. When the radio

and, like overdressing in public places, indicates that they have no other place to show their finery. People of position never put on formal evening dress on a steamer, not even in the à-la-carte restaurant. No gentleman wears a tailcoat on shipboard under any circumstances whatsoever.'

On the other hand, as Lucius Beebe has recorded: 'It was an age when the dinner jacket was not in universal accceptance among Englishmen as evening attire, and one's steward, on instructions from the bridge, laid out smoking or tails as the Commodore might have decreed ... You didn't dine at your convenience but the Commodore's and on evenings of the Captain's Dinner full evening dress was

broke the news, the *Ile* was in mid-ocean. As the prices fell 'the Companie de St. Phalle telegrapher and the *Ile de France* radio operators all worked twenty-four hour shifts, sending the endless flood of sell orders to a Stock Exchange where no one was buying. And for three days the gentlemen who were no longer interested in dinner parties or in dancing stood silent in the hall during Exchange hours, watching the figures scrawled on a blackboard that meant their fortunes were being wiped out ... bewildered and helpless in the face of catastrophe.'

Even so, for half a generation of travellers, the *Ile* would undoubtedly spell *joie de vivre*. Meanwhile, coming up in favour and, shortly, with its magnificent *Bremen*, to snatch the Blue Riband by about two knots from *Mauretania*, was Germany's Norddeutscher Lloyd. The other lines, splendid though some of their ships were, eager though they were to please, were mostly also-rans: their services tended to be slower, duller or less frequent; or, regrettably, they terminated in countries on the edge of or beyond the circles of fashion, high finance and nose-in-the-air frummery.

However, 'one of the smaller countries, Sweden, made history in 1925 when she put the first motorship into the North Atlantic passenger trade, the 17,000-ton *Gripsholm*'. This liner, named after Sweden's most famous royal castle, had a lounge 'noteworthy for its serene dignity which is achieved by means of beautifully carved mahogany, rose draperies and gilt panels. The smoke room is a reproduction of the "Astraksalen", the show place of Gripsholm Castle, the beams and walls are of silver oak, the rich carpeting and luxurious furniture give this beautiful room the atmosphere of the passengers' favourite club. There are suites-de-luxe and all the cabin accommodation is roomy and beautifully fitted.' As for the Americans the best *they* could offer on the prestigious New York–Southampton route was another ex-German, the humdrum, impersonal *Leviathan*, which ran alone and dry as it was fated to be faithfully in service during the Prohibition period.

Left: The world's largest graving dock receives as its first visitor the world's largest liner: the British liner *Majestic* enters the King George V dock at Southampton in 1934.

Far left: Reception area and main lounge of some stupendous, deluxe hotel? No: this is a scene on board the giant British transatlantic liner *Majestic* in the late 1920s.

Left: The quietly luxurious Swedish liner *Gripsholm*, the first motorship on the North Atlantic run, approaches New York at the end of its maiden voyage in 1925.

Even less *comme il faut*, but a potent sign of times to come and by no means dry, was that new ship of the air the *Graf Zeppelin* in which, as Brinnin tells us: 'Fifty passengers could be carried in two-berth staterooms, each equipped with washstands providing hot and cold running water. They could spend air-borne days in a reading and writing room, a lounge and bar, and dine at one sitting in a gallery. They could stroll on promenade decks placed on either side of the airship and they had access to shower baths.' However, the airship's fittings were 'coldly practical and without class'.

The great ocean liners, far below, ploughing their familiar furrows, were unperturbed. To their owners and their captains the world was still, and would ever be, their oyster. To their passengers, there could be no substitute for the wonder and romance of these great ships. Sinclair Lewis' Sam Dodsworth on his way to Europe in the 32,000-ton ss *Ultima* 'explored the steamer. It was to him

... the most sure and impressive mechanism he had ever seen; more satisfying than a Rolls, a Delauney-Belleville, which to him had been the equivalent of a Velasquez. He marveled at the authoritative steadiness with which the bow mastered the waves; at the powerful sweep of the lines of the deck and the trim stowage of cordage. He admired the first officers, casually pacing the bridge. He wondered that in this craft which was, after all, but a floating iron egg-shell, there should be the roseate music room, the smoking-room with its Tudor fireplace – solid and terrestrial as a castle – and the swimming pool, green-lighted water washing beneath Roman pillars. He climbed the boat deck, and some never realized desire for sea-faring was satisfied as he looked along the sweep of gangways, past the huge lifeboats, the ventilators like giant saxophones, past the lofty funnels serenely dribbling black woolly smoke, to the forward mast.'

Before the start of the 1930s, faced with the need before long to replace the 'Big Three', Cunard were working on their grand design which, ultimately, would take the form of the two most illustrious transatlantic liners, the *Queen Mary* and the *Queen Elizabeth*. These ships, larger than their predecessors, each of around 80,000 tons, with three and two funnels respectively, and a service speed of almost 30 knots, were to maintain the weekly Cunard service between New York and Southampton. The *Queen Mary*'s keel would be duly laid at the end of 1930 but, owing to the Depression, it would be May 1936 before she could make her début.

Meanwhile, with their own mammoth liner *Normandie*, the French Line stole a march, the maiden voyage taking place in May 1935. This vessel, 'with her three enormous funnels and smooth external lines which swept with Gallic aplomb from bow to stern of the largest hull ever to have been set afloat' offered 'ten *suites de luxe* and four *suites de grande luxe*', the latter having dining-rooms as well as sitting-rooms; and two of these, 'named "Deauville" and "Trouville", had no mere verandahs, but private decks'. Second in size, in due course, to *Queen Elizabeth*, the design concepts of the *Normandie* 'were immense ... yet a delicacy of line compensated for size ... The great lounge and equally spacious smoking room ... could be merged into one enormous salon ... The dining saloon was a *tour de force* of tinted glass ... longer than the famed Hall of Mirrors at Versailles ... The huge main doors were gilt over bronze and led out to a stairway that swept up to an entrance vestibule lined with Algerian onyx.'

All the major shipping lines were by now, once again, in the race, hurrying to offer a new generation of ships, new routes, new incentives, new attractions. Among many beautiful vessels, the Italian *Rex* and *Conte di Savoia*, introduced in 1932, 'went back to the grand age of Italian baroque'. According to Robert Wall, 'the ceiling of the

Britain's *Queen Mary*, perhaps the best-known liner of them all: (left) an artist's impression of this huge ship, towering above her escorting tugs; and (above) a drawing of the vessel superimposed upon London's Trafalgar Square, stern in Charing Cross Road and bow in Whitehall.

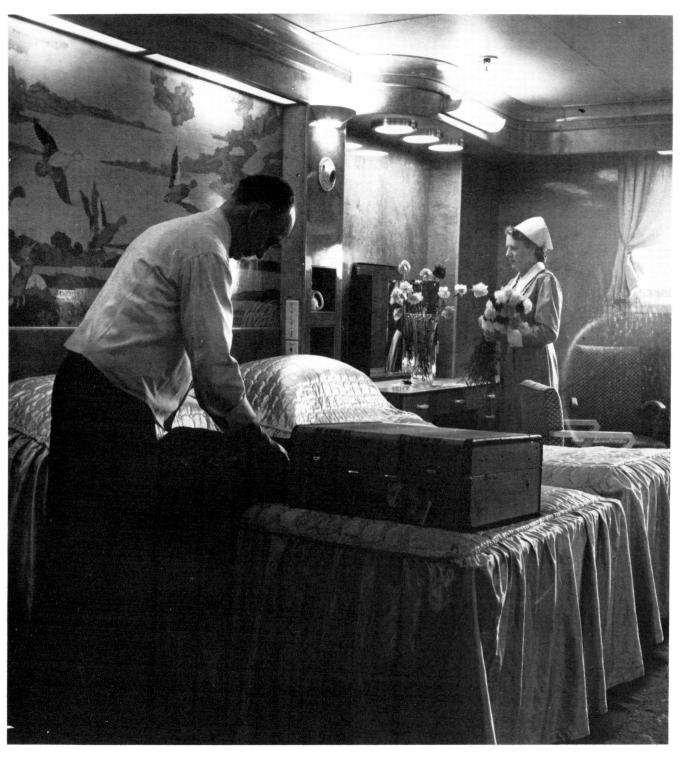

Two tantalizing glimpses of *Queen Mary*'s sumptuous
accommodation: a corner of the music room (right); and one of the
state-rooms (above) in which a steward unpacks for a newly-arrived
passenger while the stewardess arranges a vase of flowers.

The mammoth *Normandie*, pride of France's transatlantic fleet in the
mid-1930s, manoeuvring in harbour.

Opposite: Epitome of those grand days of travel, a chauffeur-driven
Mercedes of the late 1920s, with passengers in evening attire, sets off
from the quayside in the shadow of a great ocean liner.

Some forms of travel were regarded as a stage for wealthy people to perform on. This French fashion-plate of the 1930s shows two flappers all at sea in their '*pyjamas de bateau*'.

At the destination, what was there to do? Between *le déjeuner* and *le five o'clock* every well-dressed traveller *must* see the sights, of course. A Brussels scene of 1926.

Part of a private suite on board the *Normandie* (left) while (below) shows the bronze doors at one end of this liner's lavish lounge.

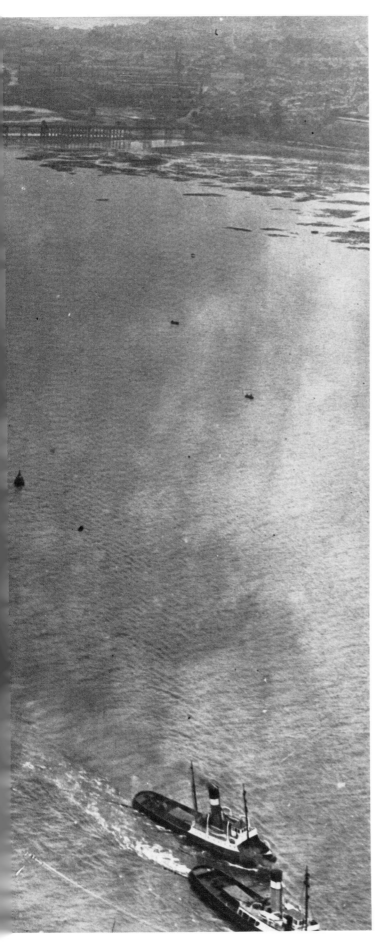

Conte would not have disgraced the Sistine Chapel', while the Dutch *Nieuw Amsterdam*, joining the throng in 1938, was to become yet another favourite of the regular traveller.

Meanwhile, the days of Prohibition past, the Americans were well into the game with their highly successful, though much smaller, *Manhattan* and *Washington*. These ships attempted the difficult feat of providing 'period' luxury at moderate prices. And, as though busy New York was not gateway enough to the United States, Canadian Pacific's luxury liner *Empress of Britain* (1931), the largest ship ever employed on the route from Britain to Canada, offered such a high speed 'that a traveller by way of Montreal could get to Chicago more quickly than by way of New York'.

Two 1930s views of the luxury liner *Empress of Britain*, the largest ship ever employed on the route from Britain to Canada, with a speed offering a faster transit through Montreal to Chicago than by the more usual route through New York.

Above: By the early 1930s the Germans had put two very fine, fast and distinguished ships into the North Atlantic service: *Bremen*, which snatched the Blue Riband from *Mauretania*, and (illustrated here) *Europa*.

Far right: The Italian superliners *Rex* and *Conte di Savoia*, plying the 'sunshine' route, were two of the most beautiful ships connecting Europe with New York in the 1930s.

Right: Among the many mixed passenger-cargo liners serving the South Atlantic was this trim German vessel *General Osorio*, photographed from a low-flying airship on an opposite course.

But it was the *Queen Mary* which, over the years, would capture the hearts and hold the memories of a generation of transatlantic travellers. With accommodation for over two thousand passengers (for up to twenty thousand whilst engaged as a troop transport during the Second World War) and, in peacetime, with every conceivable facility for their comfort, safety and enjoyment, the *Queen Mary* was both a leader of the pack and a mirror of the times.

The richer passengers would each have with them up to twenty trunks and valises; and one quarter of the passenger list was often made up of maids and other servants. Rosina Harrison recalls: 'I remember Mr Dean who had been under-butler to the Astors . . . telling me how when he was butler to Prince and Princess Obolensky, he found he was always kept busy running errands for them when he went first-class. My opportunity came when I had to go and book to go to America. Six servants were travelling, me as butler/valet, a Russian chef, a footman, Mollie, Princess Alice's maid, a nanny and a nursery maid, and my lady was complaining at the price of the tickets. "It would save you money if your maid and I travelled tourist", I quickly said, and it was agreed that we should. Well, I had the time of my life for the first half of the voyage, with the run of the bars and the run of the girls.

'Then one morning when we were splicing the main-brace someone came in and said, "Your lady's outside looking for you". Well, I slipped out of the bar . . . into the Prince's room and started busying myself. She came in a few minutes later and made a little sniffing noise. "You're travelling first-class from now on". She handed me a ticket with my cabin number. "And here's another for Mollie" – her maid. No more high jinks for us on that voyage: we had to be at her beck and call from then onwards.'

Phillips-Birt reminds us that 'the luxury liners had a ratio of servers to served of about 1:3, which is comparable with European hotels run in the grand manner. The purely domestic staff in one liner was composed thus: head waiters, 2; assistant head-waiters, 2; barmen, 6; assistant barmen, 112; stewards, 106; musicians, 11; wardrobe keepers, 3; starchers and ironers, 3; tailor's presser, 1; laundryman, 1; ladies' hairdressers, 2; barbers, 5 . . . The kitchen staff . . . would alone number much the same as the complement of seamen.' And there were gardeners, too, to tend the flowers.

On a single voyage with 2,000 passengers the assembled gullets would receive, among many other goodies, 2,500 bottles of whisky, 3,000 of table wines and 48,000 of mineral water; 75 oxen and 110 sheep; 500lb of smoked

Two pictures of *Queen Mary*'s launching party at London's Trocadero restaurant in 1936 show where some of the inspiration for this liner's interior design came from. Indeed, such were the similarities, that the photo library's original caption for the above picture describes a view of the ship's first-class dining-room; or perhaps someone was seeing double?

salmon, and 4,000 oysters; more than 5,000 chickens, ducks, turkeys and other fowl, and 70,000 eggs; 2,500 artichokes, a ton of onions and 300 tins of mushrooms; 1,000 jars of jam and 2,000 gallons of ice cream: not to mention a mere 15,000 cigars and a million or so cigarettes.

The *Queen Mary*'s opulence, bordering on ostentation, did not find universal favour. Art critic Raymond Mortimer has written about her: 'A super-luxury transatlantic liner depends largely on the patronage of international film stars, financiers, and opera singers and their taste is presumably reflected in the international style of decoration which you find in the palatial hotels all over the world from Palm Beach to the Lido.' 'Ugh!' said an English columnist, 'shiny rayon damask ... engraved Dianas with streaming hair and big-eyed unicorns racing across mirrors. Hideously patterned carpets. Strip-lit Winter Gardens with rubber plants.' 'The general effect,' said the *Architect and Building News*, 'is one of mild but expensive vulgarity.' To a London columnist she was 'a riot of ostentation carefully executed in the Leicester Square style'. However, according to Doris Zinkeisen, who designed it, the Verandah Grill was to be 'the centre of sophistication in the ship ... the rendezvous for the smart set at lunchtime ... the night club in the evening'.

When the present author crossed the Atlantic in the *Queen Mary* in the early 1960s, little seemed to have changed. 'This voyage in the *Queen Mary* being my third transatlantic passage by Cunard in three years, I knew more or less what to expect. Yet, once again, the old magic gripped me. I felt like the favourite son come home again. I was struck on the one hand by the brutish décor, on the other by the magnificent scale of the public amenities; by the almost amateurish clumsiness of the social events in contrast with the quietly confident service; by that feeling of complete security, to which one surrenders oneself without a moment's hesitation.'

He surmised that, in some respects, the routine for passengers has changed little from that 'concocted by the P & O Company in the nineties for the entertainment of inebriated rubber planters returning East after home leave ... Cunard's foreign competitors, for the most part, offer subtly compèred night-life which seems soignée, suave, spontaneous, romantic ... But steadfast Cunard ...' Well, 'many Britons, after all, prefer their night-life to be athletic, if not boisterous. The Americans ... find a reassurance, a "kinda cute" treatment in Cunard ships, to which they return time and again. And our Continental cousins ... cannot resist the chance occasionally to gaze in awe and wonder at the stolid, amateur British, stiff with pride and tradition, playing affable host in their weighty, trusty, salt-encrusted liners.'

A few years later the present author took one more trip in the *Queen Mary*, towards the end of her active life. The occasion was a short pleasure cruise, but the rituals remained the same. 'The ship's bells summoned us to lifeboat stations. An officer spoke to us on the captain's behalf, warning us kindly but firmly of the ocean's perils. Cigarettes thrown overboard might enter an open porthole and burn a bunk – or ignite its occupant; children climbing on the rail would end their days in Davy Jones's locker; in emergency we had only to collect our life-jackets and report promptly but calmly at our proper station, and all would be well.'

On the first morning at sea 'the ship was rolling lazily. My attentive cabin steward brought breakfast on a tray – fruit, crisp fresh-baked rolls, coffee with cream. Cooked dishes, cereals, juices – all were on call for the asking ... A copy of the ship's newspaper, pushed under the cabin door, brought word from the outside world. The gaily-printed programme for the day offered a tantalising array of fun and entertainment ... deck games, keep-fit hikes, a children's party, a get-together beat session for teenagers, organ music in the lounge, a string trio in the Neptune bar, the accordion in the Observation lounge.' In the late evening it was 'on with the Ladies' Night Dance. "Ladies!" shrieked the printed programme, "this is your chance to ask the gentlemen to dance." Every female was handed a dance programme, with blank spaces in which to write her intended victims' names. A few gentlemen crept stealthily out of the lounge, to take refuge in the bars, but most remained, eyes downcast with becoming modesty.'

Finally, on the homeward stretch, it was Gala Night. 'Garlands between the pillars, streamers, netted balloons awaiting their release, spot lights, fairy lights, a Cole Porter foxtrot, the thronged dance floor ... then, as the dance orchestra took its well-earned tea break, a lively long-haired loud-playing beat group mounted the stage ...

Mini-skirted teenagers and young-twenties jerked and gyrated prettily upon the floor while their elders, firmly seated, nodded benign if uncomprehending approval ... the orchestra returned to its duty ... Midnight. On to the Neptune bar night club. Dimmer lights, cosier atmosphere, sultrier music ... A few gulps of sea air. Full moon, dappling the quiet sea. And so, down the deserted stairway to my cabin – and bed-time for me.'

And so, also, back to earth. 'We have just turned into Southampton water, after steaming close to the lush green northern shore of the Isle of Wight, with Ryde and Cowes to port, Portsmouth to starboard. It is a bright, crisp, windy morning. The great roadstead of Spithead, once a meeting point of Britain's ironclad armadas, seemed strangely deserted. A solitary destroyer circled languidly, tracking a phantom submarine. A lone yachtsman in yellow wind-cheater, scudding along under reefed mainsail, passed close by our towering ship and waved his greeting.

'We pause off the pilot vessel to allow the harbour pilot in his plunging tender to come on board. Now, to port,

Fawley refinery, that dense forest of silvery shapes and structures. And ahead, the long waterfront of Southampton docks coming nearer, splashes of colour under the tall cranes emerging gradually into the distinct forms of sleek elegant liners awaiting their departures to faraway continents. The *Old Lady*, with her retinue of tugs and launches, moving at a fair speed, turns smartly towards her berth, hesitates, and runs neatly in, without fuss, to rest gently against the catamarans. Friends and well-wishers wave from the observation platform, bunting streams out in the wind, and great hawsers quiver under the power of the winches, come taut and are made fast ... Down to the restaurant for our last lunch, served briskly by smiling stewards.' In the lounge, afterwards, a last look round. 'The great tall room is almost empty, chairs and tables stacked to await the cleaners, the stage bare. We seem already to have joined the *Old Lady*'s silent company of ghosts to sail on into the future until, finally, she is rent apart and scattered among the scrapyards, her secrets wafted into oblivion by the mourning winds.'

Three decades before, albeit for different reasons, the same sad sense of foreboding prevailed. The curtain was about to rise for the final, brave but short-lived act of the great transatlantic pageant. In 1940, as Brinnin has recorded, 'tethered to Manhattan like circus animals with no place to go, the great liners – *Ile de France, Normandie, Queen Mary, Queen Elizabeth, Aquitania, Rex* – lightly rose and fell with the tides of the Hudson. Then, one by one, refitted and reduced to anonymous shades of military gray, they were sent off on missions of war. In a sense, they would never come back again. The concours d'élégance was over; the golden rosettes and silver loving cups had all been awarded.'

And soon to be over, too, those poignantly romantic occasions for friends and relations waving their goodbyes across a widening gap of water, through the splash of the final hawser, the trailing end of the last paper streamer, to the moment when familiar faces high up on the boat deck go out one by one, like small lights in a distant building. Departures have never been the same again.

Life on board. The caption given to the cabin scene (seen here) in 1931 was, dramatically: 'This is the first time that Intimate Pictures have been taken aboard a big liner.'

Less inhibited, apart from the headgear, is the Roaring Twenties view of couples dancing energetically on *Aquitania*'s promenade deck.

Grand days away from it all: a scrapbook miscellany.

R.M.S.
"QUEEN MARY"

R.M.S.

"QUEEN MARY"

Quadruple-Screw Turbine ... Gross Tonnage 80,773

LIST OF OFFICERS

Commodore—Sir EDGAR BRITTEN, R.D., R.N.R.

Staff Captain—B. H. DAVIES, O.B.E., R.D., R.N.R.

Chief Engineer.........L. ROBERTS	Chief Officer...C. G. ILLINGWORTH R.D., R.N.R.
Staff Chief Engineer W. SUTCLIFFE	Purser..............C. G. JOHNSON R.D., R.N.R.
Physician and Principal Medical Officer..............G. A. GOOLDEN	Staff Purser..........L. E. CARINE
Surgeon.............E. C. BUTLER F.R.C.S.	Chief Steward..........A. E. JONES

Company's Representative— E. SEYMOUR-BELL

Ocean Times

PUBLISHED ON BOARD CUNARD WHITE STAR LINERS

Sunday, October 25, 1936	R.M.S. AQUITANIA	North Atlantic Edition

RESULT OF CIANO'S MEETING WITH HITLER

GERMANY FORMALLY DECIDES TO RECOGNISE THE ITALIAN ETHIOPIAN EMPIRE

'BERLIN.—The simultaneous publication in Berlin and Rome that the Reich has formally decided to recognise the Italian Empire of Ethiopia is the only tangible result of Italian Foreign Minister Ciano's meeting with Reichsfuehrer Hitler so far, but it is not necessarily the only result reached, states the "Sunday Times" correspondent.

In view of Premier Mussolini's close personal control of the Italian foreign policy, any further proposals by Hitler for reciprocation could not be answered on the spot by Count Ciano.

It is understood that such recognition and its corollary of mutual recognition of the Franco Government, as soon as Madrid falls, was decided upon before Ciano left Rome.

Italy, generally, greets the decision with joy, and while the man-in-the-street anticipates that Britain and France will follow Hitler's example, responsible quarters hold the view that there will not be any change.

Berlin hints at further co-operation in aliance with France

MUSSOLINI'S "MESSAGE OF PEACE"

"OLIVE BRANCH IN FOREST OF BAYONETS"

BOLOGNA.—Premier Mussolini, thundering out a "message of peace" in this city, where he narrowly escaped assassination ten years ago, yesterday thrust before the world "an olive branch growing out of an immense forest of eight million well-sharpened bayonets in the hands of youths of dauntless heart."

He told 100,000 Bolognese he desired to "launch a message which should go beyond the mountains and hills."

"It is a message of peace," peace in work and work in peace," he shouted from the gorgeously decorated Piazza.

Recalling the achievements of Fascism in the ten years since he last visited Bologna, he declared "People such as the Italian people, heirs to an ancient and magnificent civilisation, have car-

NEWS IN BRIEF

LONDON.—The death occurred yesterday of Viscountess Elibank (93), the mother of the present Peer.

LONDON.— Weather report: bright periods; minimum temperature 47, maximum 56; sunshine, 3.9 hours.

TYRONE. — Lieut.-Colonel J. K. McClintock, A.D.C. to the Governor of North Ireland, the Earl of Abercorn, was found dead in bed yesterday.

OSLO (Reuter).—The Defence Minister has granted a two years' concession to Aberdeen Airways for an Aberdeen-Stavanger route, opening in April.

ALAMEDA, CAL. — A 17-day transPacific air odyssey ended yesterday when the China Clipper arrived to complete its 16,000 mile preliminary passenger round-trip flight to Manila.

LONDON.—Lawn Tennis: The Surrey Covered Courts Championship resulted: Women's singles: Miss James beat Fraulein Rose, 6—4, 6—3. Men's singles: Wilde beat Ellmer, 6—4, 6—4.

BROOKLANDS—The hangars at this

MOTIF IN ANODYSED ALUMINIUM BY MAURICE LAMBERT.
MAIN DECK—R.M.S. "QUEEN MARY".

R.M.S. "QUEEN MARY"   WEDNESDAY, JUNE 10, 1936

Breakfast

FRUITS

Preserved Ginger   Baked Apples   Compôte of Apricots
Stewed Figs   California Figs in Syrup   Compôte of Prunes
Honey Dew Melon   Grape Fruit   Pears   Cantaloup
Apples   Oranges   Bananas   Prune Juice
Orange Juice   Tomato Juice   Grape Fruit Juice

CEREALS

Oatmeal   Quaker Oats   Cream of Wheat   Farina
Bonny Boy Toasted Oats   Creamed Barley   All Bran
Post Toasties   Puffed Rice   Force Whole-Wheat Flakes
Shredded Wheat   Bran Flakes   Grape Nuts

TO ORDER (10 minutes)—Onion Soup Gratinée

FISH

Fried Porgies, Anchovy Sauce   Halibut Portugaise
London Haddie in Cream   Kippered Herrings
Butterfish Meunière

EGGS AND OMELETTES

Eggs—Boiled, Fried, Turned, Poached, Scrambled and Buttered
Shirred Eggs Princesse   Omelettes—Cheese, Jelly and Tomato

ENTREES

Minced Chicken and Red Peppers   Kidney Sauté Madère
Pan-Fried Dry Hash Cakes

GRILLS

Ham Steaks, Devilled Sauce   Duck's Legs Savora
Tomato and Fresh Pork Sausage   Tomatoes
Pale and Smoked Wiltshire, American and Irish Bacon
York and Wiltshire Ham

POTATOES

Sauté   Mashed   French Fried   Maître d'Hôtel

COLD MEATS ASSORTED

SALADS

Tomatoes   Watercress   Spring Onions   Radishes

CAKES

Buckwheat   Griddle   Waffles   Maple or Golden Syrup

BREADS, Etc.

French   Graham   Brioche   Crescents   Oatcake   Rolls
Currant   Hövis   Cottage   Corn   Soda Scones
Cream Scones   Triscuits   French Toast

PRESERVES

Strawberry   Raspberry   Plum   Damson   Apricot   Black Currant
Red Currant Jelly   Honey   Honey in the Comb   Marmalade
Grape Fruit Marmalade   Lime Marmalade

BEVERAGES

Tea—Indian, China, Ceylon, Linden and Camomile   Coffee
Cadbury's Cup Chocolate   Horlick's Malted Milk—Plain or Chocolate
Cocoa   Instant Postum   Kaffee Hag Coffee

Passengers on Special Diet are requested to make known their requirements
to the Head Waiter

Cunard
White Star

PRINTED IN ENGLAND   Q.C.8.2

3 OCEAN TRAVEL: SINEWS OF EMPIRE

A new experience for transatlantic passengers: the soda fountain on board *Aquitania* in the 1920s when even to suck a straw was something a lady did in style.

In the summer of 1937 a young naval officer in London was preparing for a spell of foreign service. His destination was Hong Kong where he was to join a destroyer and so become part of the long-established British naval presence in the Far East. According to the rules and custom of that period he would be away from his home country, his family and his friends for some two and a half years: thus, the preparations, the assembly of kit and chattels, the settlement of debts and all the farewells needed time.

The port of departure was Southampton, the conveyance being a new British India liner, *Dunera*, doing duty as a troopship. The embarkation process, described by the present author in his book *No More Heroes*, 'needed two porters at the station to handle my baggage. I had with me the standard outfit for a British sub-lieutenant going overseas, packed in a hefty wooden chest, a trunk, a large

metal case, a couple of suitcases, a helmet box and a golf-bag full of clubs, sword and walking sticks. The gear included epaulettes, frock-coat, sword-belt and gold-striped trousers for ceremonial occasions; blue uniform suits for cool weather and white ones for hot; shoulder-strapped shirts and white shorts for day wear in the tropics; short uniform jackets, blue and white, for evening wear on duty; a tail suit, a dinner jacket and a white tuxedo for smart civilian evenings; stiff and soft white shirts, butterfly collars, black and white bow ties; plain clothes and sports attire for all weathers; a cocked hat, uniform caps, civilian hats and the blessed helmet; an accompanying variety of footwear; books, underwear, pyjamas, a first-aid kit and a telescope. The survival of the Empire was at stake, no less.'

Although the passenger list on this occasion comprised naval, military and air force personnel travelling on duty,

the amenities and service in first and second class were the same as those available to fare-paying passengers when, during the non-trooping season, the ship plied the seas in the civilian capacity for which, in the main, she was designed. As a troopship first class was for officers and, apart from a shortage of women, children and elderly people, the passengers were much the same as those to be found in any liner sailing the same route. And they were there for much the same reason: the wish or the need to go abroad to earn their living, while furthering their employers' interests, in one or other of the imperial dependencies. Thus, the great shipping lines connecting Europe with India and beyond depended very largely for their passenger traffic on contracts with government or with large-scale employers: unlike the transatlantic traffic, few passengers on the imperial-liner routes were there for

One of the liners of Britain's dependable P & O company on the Europe–Suez Canal–Far East run in the 1930s was *Strathaird*, seen here at anchor off Bombay.

show, pleasure or regardless of expense.

Travelling second class on board *Dunera* were the non-commissioned officers: the petty officers and sergeants. They too, in their separate, self-contained accommodation, enjoyed the same treatment as the second-class passengers would at other times; and by and large this was a cut above the comforts which awaited them in their quarters in warship or barracks overseas. For the other ranks, for the ordinary sailors, soldiers and airmen, however, it was a rather different story.

As we learn from *Plain Tales from the Raj*, 'the British troops went out on small over-crowded "vomit-buckets" ... The officers got three-quarters of the ship with their lounges and smoke rooms and luxurious cabins, and the troops got only the troop-deck ... The unfortunate ones had to pick up their baggage and get up on deck, a favourite place being round the funnel, where it was warm, or under the boat deck ... No one came round to see that the latrines were working ... You couldn't get into a wash place, you couldn't get to your kit and worst of all, you couldn't get to your hammock.'

So, down below *Dunera*'s gleaming promenade decks – below the carpeted bars and lounges, the plush state-rooms and cabins with their portholes looking out on the sparkling seas, the restaurants with white-coated stewards laying up the tables – were the large, dark, ill-ventilated holds of a vessel which, when not trooping, was intended for mixed trade duties, for the carriage of cargoes as well as of passengers. Where the cargoes were stowed on civilian journeys, other ranks were put on trooping trips. The difference between the classes was no less marked on deck: the other ranks were confined to small areas at the extreme ends of the ship while those in first and second class – relatively few in number – lorded it in spacious style over the hot, crowded yet ever-cheerful lesser mortals in accommodation of barely steerage standard.

Yet when the ship, during its five-week voyage, called at the various ports en route, Gibraltar, Malta, Port Said, Suez, Aden, Bombay, Colombo and Singapore, and shore-leave was given, all these men would emerge spruce, clean, immaculately uniformed, and walk the streets with dignity as befitted their role as representatives of the great raj. Officers and their men alike, when they went ashore or about their duties in foreign parts, small islands of self-confidence in the swirling sea of dark-skinned local inhabitants, there was no doubt about who was master and who was servant.

So it was, thus it had been for many years and long, if not forever, would it last. The edifice looked firm and permanent; and one vital component was the stepping-stones laid over the decades by the British, dominant among the imperial powers, to mark their well-trodden path from West to East. *Dunera*'s ports of call, between one thousand and two thousand miles apart, a distance governed mainly by the endurance of the earlier steamships plying the route, served several purposes. Foremost was their role as coaling, latterly oiling, stations with stocks always available for the bunkers of warships as well as of troopships, liners and tramp steamers. But these stocks, and the colliers or tankers crossing the seas to replenish them, needed protection, so each of these ports was also a defended naval base and garrison town. In turn, these functions led to the establishment of communities of people whose livelihood and way of life depended on the continued presence of the imperial masters and, increasingly, of their wives and families too. And, from these beginnings, a trading activity would invariably ensue, most of these ports becoming a gateway for merchandise entering or leaving the hinterland and, usually, a centre of administration, finance and communications for the area.

Although the character of each port and of its inhabitants differed there were so many features in common that the itinerant Briton, although far from home, felt himself to be on familiar ground. The Union Jack flew prominently above the fort, the arrival ceremonies and disembarkation processes were always the same, unobtrusive policemen were a reassurance that the prevailing ambience of law and order had substance, and, wherever the white man walked, the streets were clean, the grass was green and the natives, if not begging favours, smiled amiably and stood aside.

At sea, the day-by-day routine on board *Dunera* varied little. An Indian steward, after knocking on the door, entered the roomy, well ventilated, twin-bedded state-room which our young sub-lieutenant shared with a colleague, opened the curtain to let the sunlight stream in through the porthole, laid out fresh towels by the handbasin and poured cups of tea ready for the masters' pleasure. In answer to a bedside bell, the bathroom steward, another Indian, white teeth gleaming in an eager-to-please smile, came in to receive instructions for the running of the morning bath; and when this was done, with large bath towels and fresh soap at the ready, the steward returned, reported and withdrew.

Cunard's famous record-breaking *Mauretania*, the 'grand old lady of the Atlantic', held by thousands in affectionate esteem, seen here in 1935 at the end of its long years of service.

The German liner *Imperator* which, ceded to Britain after the First World War, became Cunard's *Berengaria* and was regarded by many in the 1920s as the most opulent liner in the North Atlantic.

In the 1930s the French transatlantic liners vied with Cunard in style and elegance with elaborate, sophisticated settings aimed at the Western world's most fashionable women and their wealthy escorts. These artists' impressions show: (below) a sumptuous corner of *L'Atlantique*'s vast, soaring first-class lounge; (above) the same ship's temple-like swimming pool, where even in their bathing costumes the ladies resembled well-coiffed goddesses.

In the large, quietly elegant first-class restaurant, where the sub-lieutenant shared a corner table with five shipmates, another posse of stewards, supervised by Europeans, hurried obediently about their hungry passengers' business. A full English breakfast included bacon, ham, fish and every kind of egg dish; fruit juices or cereals; toast or rolls with honey or marmalade; tea or coffee or, for those hung-over, a horse's neck, or a prairie oyster: all were on call if not on the printed menu.

During the forenoon, for the officers in first class there were only two events to distinguish this trooping voyage from those of the ship in her civilian role: a forty-minute lecture on a military subject by a senior officer, and a twenty-minute PT session. The rest of every day was entirely free except that each officer-passenger would be listed for some minor official duty, usually including a round of inspection of the other ranks' quarters, about every sixth or seventh day.

It was, therefore, a question of deck games, dice, cards; walking the decks or a swim in the ship's pool; iced drinks served by stewards in the lounge, bars or shady corners up on deck. Then, lunch, a two-hour ritual with its gargantuan choice of dishes, marked conspicuously by expertly made, highly spiced curry dishes; a siesta, then more exercise; a tombola session, a film show, books to return to the library, letters to be written home, a quiet chat with friends. And so into evening gear, stiff-fronted (in the tropics, soft-fronted) shirt, butterfly collar, black bowtie, serge (in the tropics, white drill) mess jacket with rank markings, well-pressed, well-tailored trousers, black shoes. A short walk on deck in the gathering dusk, a round or two of cocktails and down to the restaurant for another vastly elaborate four- or five-course meal accompanied by sherry, then wine, beer or whisky, with port or brandy and, perhaps, a cigar to follow. Music from the ship's orchestra during dinner and afterwards in the first-class lounge though, alas, with limited opportunity for dancing, this passenger list's female element comprising only a handful of wives of senior officers and a sprinkling of military nurses.

But the scene in *Dunera*'s softly lit public rooms, with their chintz-covered sofas in the lounge and leather armchairs in the bars, was a microcosm of the British ruling-class way of life the world over. Whether in club, mess or wardrobe, in verandahed residence or governor's ball-room, the laconic mien of the men in their evening clothes, the active, fresh-faced women, the genial yet oddly affected chat laced with careful banter, the polite but definite way with servants, the evident self-assurance: here, in all these familiar forms, in their familiar settings, was the thinly spread cement which held together the vast, stable but quietly seething commonwealth so widespread that the sun, it was said, could never set upon it.

While each port was thus, to an extent, a recognizable link in the imperial chain, the differences of character were not to do merely with changing physical and racial characteristics. Each port was one step further from home and each port added, in its own way, to the growing wonder at the size, variety and mystique of the Empire.

The Orient, which began at Port Said, cast a special spell on all who travelled into it and through it by sea in those days, and the further the ship steamed beyond Suez the more this intoxicating glamour gripped the traveller. The more also did the experience tend to bolster the white man's ego and, in the case of their excellencies, as of the managers and officers, the top of the heap in their own countries also, reinforce their certainties and override their doubts. Five weeks out of Southampton and the *Dunera*'s passengers, eagerly lining the rails as the ship sidled into its berth in Hong Kong, were in all respects ready for their role.

The civilian shipping lines which formed the sinews of empire, in their civilian as well as in their trooping roles, drew from and contributed to the clear-cut demarcation lines between the ranks and classes within the white communities and between the communities, white and native. Nowhere was this game played more assiduously than in the splendid liners of the British P & O Company, whose ships were, indeed, in their hemisphere, the élite of an élite. As its full name implies, the Peninsular and Oriental Steam Navigation Company began life in trade between Britain, Spain and Portugal; and although presented with a fairly clear opportunity, the Company for many years resisted the temptation to extend its operations beyond the Mediterranean. The breakthrough came in 1840 when, after pressure from the British authorities in India, the Company entered into a contract to provide a regular mail service, including an overland hop across Egypt. Before that time dispatches between England and India could be up to six months in transit, and this meant that a year or so might pass before any reply to a letter could be received.

At first the few passengers who travelled the new P & O route could hardly regard the experience as a holiday. As Boyd Cable recalled in his book *A Hundred Year History of the P & O*, part of the Egyptian stage was on the Nile by a steamer so small that it carried only ten people and 'the moving of one person was enough to trim the boat. She was of 6 horse-power (described by the wags as 3 donkey-power) and there is testimony of many travellers that she was the home of (several) species of creepy-crawly vermin.' ... Then, 'each person must take a sufficiency of bottled water for the desert crossing ... and a supply of wine and moderate amount of spirits was also recommended ... and native bread being uneatable, cabin or ship's biscuits and rusks should be carried'.

He continues by describing the food generally as 'impossible for any European to eat – the meat and chicken being incredibly tough and tasteless and only the eggs eatably tender – if those boiled to leather or bullet consistency were resolutely rejected ... The transit passengers had every chance of arriving at the landing stage for Alexandria after or near sunset; and after another transhipment to donkeys or camels ... at the city gates, to find them inexorably closed' and 'in such cases there was nothing for it but to resort to one of the low and villainous cafés and resorts outside the city walls, resolutely refuse to sit, much less lie down, and watch the locals lounge and scratch'.

The journey between England and Egypt was itself no sinecure. In 1844 a recommended route, after crossing the English Channel, comprised Ostend to Liège by train, on to Aix-la-Chapelle by coach, thence to Cologne by train, to Mainz by coach, to Basle by steamer, then over the Alps, mainly by a series of coaches, to Trieste, and so across the Mediterranean by steamer.

Comforts on board ship on the run between Egypt and India steadily improved and, in particular, victuals were provided to suit British tastes. Although these generally favoured British dishes, 'Indian curries (chicken, beef, mutton, vegetable and fish) with all due and proper accompaniments of chutney, poppadums and Bombay duck, plain or pillau-rice, were from the first regarded as one of the essential and never-to-be-missed characteristics' on P & O liners.

Even so, to quell the pangs of homesickness as well as hunger, in January 1862 P & O's *Simla* was offering its passengers an *à la carte* menu which, following mutton broth, included a choice of roast turkey, sucking pig, goose, duck and beef; boiled legs of mutton; fowl and ham pies, kidney pudding, braised sheep's head, stewed pig's feet and, last resort of the famished, corned beef. The final course of this hefty meal comprised fruit tarts, black cap pudding, sandwich pastry, apple turnovers, jam tartlets, sponge cakes, Brighton rocks, pancakes and rice puddings. Furthermore, 'all joints and poultry were brought whole to the saloon and carved there' having been fellow-passengers, alive and well, thus far; and such meals were consumed even on the hottest stretches of the voyage.

As for the heat, 'there was no adequate division between the heat of the engine-room and the passengers' quarters . . . With a following wind, the smoke from the funnels rose straight up and floated overhead in a smut and cinder-dropping cloud, and the inside of the ship everywhere was like an oven. The only relief to be obtained was when the Captain turned the ship about and steamed into the wind for a few minutes so as to get a good sweeping-through draught . . . The Red Sea was always the dreaded part of the passage . . . On the outward passage, the cabins on the port side got the early morning sun, but had the whole day to cool off . . . On the homeward passage, of course, it was reversed, and the port cabins for the worst roasting. High officials and important dignitaries were accordingly given the preference of the cooler cabins to port on the outward and to starboard on the homeward passages; and this "Port Outward – Starboard Homeward" became shortened down to the initials "P.O.S.H.", and so the favoured passengers were the "posh" ones.'

Rawalpindi, a liner in traditional P & O style and livery, and a favourite with the Sahibs and their families travelling to and from India, arrives home at Tilbury in 1933.

A forerunner of the more modern liners serving the imperial routes, this Union-Castle ship (above) leaves London for Cape Town at the turn of the century. Social life on the run to South Africa was elegantly hectic (below), that part of the world being already a holiday resort for the well-to-do.

In the circumstances, the baggage allowance was generous. 'The P & O about this date allowed first-class passengers 4 cwt. of personal baggage each ... The weight and measurements were dictated by the size, shape, and weight of a package that could be slung on a camel's back ... Imagine the tragic case of the passenger who found at the last minute that there was no "room in the vessel" for his seventy-odd shirts, his 100 pairs of socks, *and his eighteen nightcaps!*' The latter were among the many items recommended to intending Orient-bound travellers by leading outfitters of that period.

The opening of the Suez Canal in 1869 must have come as a great relief to European passengers bound for India, the Far East and Australasia. For the P & O Company, however, it was at first a mixed blessing. Their two fleets of ships, operating on either side of Egypt, were now redundant and had to be replaced with a new breed of liner suited to the through passage. Much of the infrastructure created in Egypt for the conveyance and convenience of passengers on the overland stretch also became superfluous. And the new canal, open to all users, attracted a new wave of competition, including, among others, France's Messageries Maritimes, Holland's Nederland and Rotterdam Lloyd, Italy's Italian Lines, Germany's Norddeutscher Lloyd and Japan's Nippon Yusen Kaisha.

But P & O, which continued to hold the British mail contract, adapted to the new conditions and maintained its leading position. After the First World War, in common with other shipping lines, the P & O fleet of ships was in urgent need of renewal and it is a sign of the Company's vigour that, by 1925, its fleet increased from forty-four to sixty ships – even the Depression failed to set it back. In the late 1920s and throughout the 1930s, several new liners were commissioned, of which perhaps the *Viceroy of India*, in its amenities including the provision of only single-berth cabins, was both the most beautiful and, in essence, the most traditional. Technically, however, this ship had the unusual feature of propulsion by electricity, employing a current derived from generators powered by two steam turbines; and with a speed of nearly 20 knots, this liner lowered the London–Bombay record to a transit time of just over sixteen days.

The present author remembers a homeward voyage in the *Viceroy of India* in the closing weeks of 1935. In his book *Independent Traveller* he records that 'experienced travellers preferred her to the newer vessels entering the famous service connecting Britain, through Suez, with India and the Far East'. He records that the passenger list was headed by 'a majestic Commander-in-Chief ... accompanied by mountains of baggage, a wife and an ADC ... After lunch I repaired to the lounge for coffee, choosing a pleasant table in the corner. Immediately, anxious stewards came whispering at me: if I did not mind, could I possibly sit elsewhere ... this was His Excellency's

favourite table . . . they were sure I would understand . . . '

That incident typified the rank-conscious atmosphere, which this anecdote from *Plain Tales from the Raj* brings to a comic head. There was one famous occasion on a voyage to India 'when a governor's daughter happened to be a passenger aboard the ship. The first class was full of very stuffy people and she took a fancy to a very handsome young second class steward and when the fancy-dress ball was being held she danced with him all night, and the next morning – they having parted, perhaps, only half an hour beforehand – he approached her and she froze him absolutely stiff in his tracks and said, "In the circle in which I move, sleeping with a woman does not constitute an introduction."'

Any ship is a hierarchical community but, to borrow again from *Independent Traveller*, 'the standards set to suit the highest and mightiest were, subject to protocol and to possession of a first class ticket,' available to all. Every passenger 'was pampered and had his ego stimulated to a gratifying degree . . . Everywhere servants waited to dance attendance on him – to bring him drinks, a quoit, a ping-pong ball, a paper hat; to point the way to the cinema, the gymnasium, the swimming pool . . . Repeatedly through the leisurely course of every day and night an orchestra, sweating politely under the punkah louvres, would take up its station in the palm-treed lounge, playing music to suit the moment. The grand climax in the small hours was a whirling series of old-fashioned waltzes, a gallop and finally, lights dimmed . . . that last exercise for flagging violins, "Good Night Sweetheart". Then the company would brace itself into immobility as the loyal strains of "God Save the King" floated out through the opened windows, across the moonlit decks, and away into the tropical night.'

On that occasion the ship, docking at Tilbury a few days before Christmas, brought its passengers home in time for that festival. This was just as well if only because, according to Somerset Maugham, Christmas at sea does not necessarily bring out the best of goodwill in one's fellow passengers. In *Altogether*, in a story headed 'P & O', referring to a passage from Penang to Aden around 1930, 'the passengers settled down to a pleasant voyage across the Indian Ocean. They played deck games, they gossiped about one another, they flirted . . . Someone had suggested that there should be a fancy-dress dance on Christmas day . . . A meeting was held of the first-class passengers to decide whether the second-class passengers should be invited. The ladies said that the second-class passengers would only feel ill-at-ease . . . they would drink more than was good for them and unpleasantness might ensue . . . No one would be so snobbish as to think there was any difference between first and second-class passengers as far as that went, but it would really be kinder to the second-class passengers not to put them in a false position . . . No one wanted to hurt their feelings, and of course one had to be more democratic nowadays . . . and even though they wouldn't enjoy it, they might like to come.

'Mr Gallagher was taking home in the second-class a

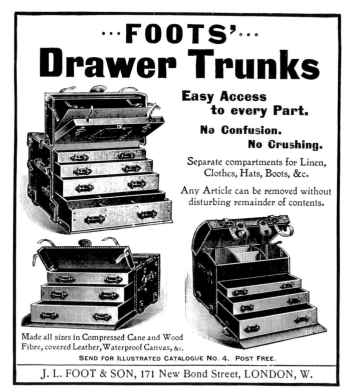
As these advertisements show, it was hardly *comme-il-faut* to travel light: the fashionable traveller, clearly, must want for nothing.

man who had been employed on his estate . . . "I've got the man who was looking after our engines with me. He's a rattling good fellow, and he's just as fit to come to your party as I am. But he won't come because I'm going to make him so drunk on Christmas day that by six o'clock he'll be fit for nothing but to be put to bed."' One hopes that he surfaced in time to go under again on New Year's Eve – a truly happy man!

While the shipping routes which converged on the Suez Canal and, after passing down the Red Sea, fanned out across the Indian Ocean, were perhaps the most spectacular sinews of empire for European powers with overseas possessions, of great importance also were those serving west, central and southern Africa, and not least South Africa. The most prominent shipping company in this trade, particularly on the direct Atlantic route, was the British Union-Castle Line. This Company, a combination of two former competitors, having enjoyed varied fortunes throughout most of the nineteenth century, came into its own, reaching new heights of prosperity with the discovery in South Africa of gold and diamonds. Although never a world leader in terms of design and luxury, its ships developed an enviable reputation for reliability, solid comfort and, from its stewards, a high standard of personal service.

After the First World War, with the RMS *Arundel Castle*

of 1921, a new era in ocean travel between Great Britain and South Africa commenced. As Marischal Murray recalls in his book *Union-Castle Chronicle*, 'her tonnage of 19,000 made the *Arundel Castle* almost half as large again as the *Balmoral Castle*, which for eleven years had been the largest vessel in the Union-Castle fleet'. The new ship 'embodied many new features in her passenger accommodation. There were suites of rooms; cabins with private bathrooms; for the first time in a mail ship there was an ample supply of single-berth cabins. Inner cabins were ventilated by a patent system of forced draught, and this meant the disappearance of the electric fan. In the first-class there was a built-in swimming pool, with gymnasium adjoining; also a passenger lift. The forward end of the promenade deck was enclosed by glass windows instead of being given uncertain protection by a canvas screen.'

Another big step forward in passenger amenity was made in the mid-1930s with the *Stirling Castle* and *Athlone Castle* in which, besides much-improved cabins, 'in the first-class there was now the "Long Gallery", a dignified apartment linking Smoking Room with Lounge, while opening off the latter was a particularly charming Drawing Room, furnished with impeccable taste. Most revolutionary, however, was the institution of a new . . . "Cabin" class . . . better than the first class in several of the older vessels'.

All this was in stark contrast with some of these ships' predecessors. In 1860, for example, second-class passengers, berthed amidships, were 'tormented by the heat of the furnaces'; and even the best cabins, located over the propeller, were furnished only with hard and narrow bunks. There were no bathrooms: 'when the decks were washed in the early morning a tub was filled with salt water and into this you jumped – between the hours of 5 am and 7 am'. No smoking was allowed below decks and, to minimize the risk of fire, little lighting was provided, that for the cabins consisting of candles 'fixed in lanterns so placed that one lantern served for two adjacent cabins, and even these were extinguished by the stewards at "lights out" around 9.30pm'.

In 1881 the Company's Chairman reported: 'We have been educated up to a standard of luxury that our forefathers never dreamt of. Even our second-class passengers want baths; they want a piano in their saloons; and they even want ice at their meals.' By the 1890s things were looking up even further. By now 'South Africa was on the way to becoming a holiday resort . . . of the leisured and more well-to-do classes . . . During the months of the Northern winter . . . the Gay Nineties were in full swing at Johannesburg'. One enthusiast wrote: 'The pursuit of pleasure is fierce and reckless . . . An English theatrical company played "Charley's Aunt" there before it reached San Francisco . . . Sometimes there is Grand Opera, and then at least fifty Society women will cable to Worth's for gowns.' The shipping line 'decided to build its own hotel in

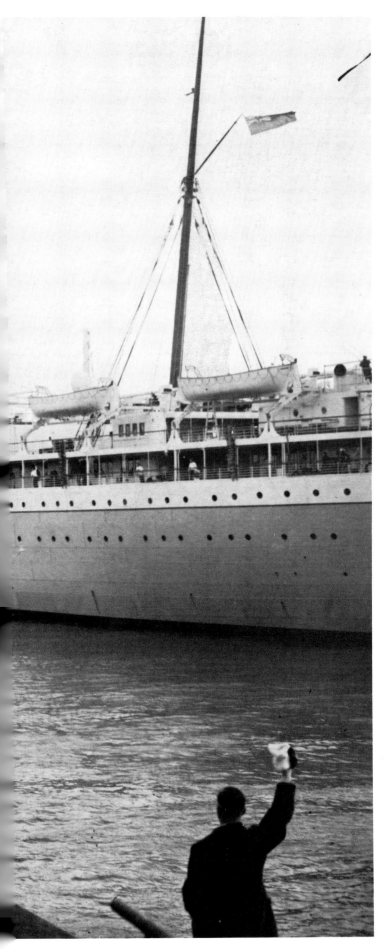

Cape Town ... It lay in the most desirable part of the city of Cape Town, at the top of the Government Avenue, near the Public Gardens ... The Mount Nelson Hotel, standing in gardens as beautiful as they were a century ago, remains one of Cape Town's oases of quiet dignity and gracious living.'

Before the First World War, 'ladies who appeared unaccompanied on deck after 10.30 p.m. – at which time deck lights were subdued – were politely asked to go inside. This meant, in effect, that they had to retire to their cabins, for lounge lights were extinguished at 10.30 and in those days no lady was permitted to enter the smoking-room.' However, 'after the War there began a gradual encroachment on the smoke-room, until by the middle Twenties ladies could no longer be barred from this one-time sanctuary of the males'.

How much further could emancipation go? In 1935, according to George Eells, Cole Porter wrote the score of *Jubilee* and more lyrics for *Anything Goes* while on a world tour with his wife Linda, who 'chanced to remark that she had always longed for an audience with the Sultan of Zanzibar but understood it was almost impossible to

The Union-Castle liner *Stirling Castle*, at that time the largest ship engaged in the South African trade, leaves Southampton on its maiden voyage via Madeira to the Cape in 1936, by now a popular route for tourists.

arrange. The impossible was a challenge Cole welcomed, and he immediately went into action, contacting both Lady Cunard and Duff Cooper.' The key to success, evidently, was Union-Castle from whom a cable was duly received: 'Audience Sultan arranged for Cole Porter party.' At the palace they found the Sultan had that morning received a ping-pong set from Lady Cunard, and two servants then carried in 'an ancient victrola, wound it up . . . and the party sat in silence as the beaming host watched them listen to a very scratchy recording of Irene Bordoni singing "Night and Day"'.

By mid-1939, after completion of a major modernization programme, the Union-Castle Line 'could claim that it possessed what was probably the most up-to-date fleet in the British Mercantile Marine'. To what avail? Eleven *Castles* were to be lost through enemy action in the Second World War and then, alas, 'little was to remain of the fine services that were in operation prior to the outbreak of hostilities'.

Although some of the world's finest ships have long crossed the Pacific along several important trade routes, this facet of the ocean-liner saga is relatively unsung. The Pacific routes, from South as well as North America, and via the Panama Canal from Europe to Japan, China, Australia and New Zealand, have been well served by numerous shipping lines. Of these, perhaps the Canadian Pacific Line deserves pride of place with its famous *Empress* series of liners, four of which were needed to maintain the required Canadian–Japanese service at peak periods. According to R M Wilson in his book *The Big Ships*, one of the most handsome of these was the 26,000-ton *Empress of Japan*, launched in 1929. She was 'designed on the most palatial lines and her public rooms, some of which were connected by a long gallery, included a central hall, glass-domed lounge, palm-court, smoking-room, card-room and writing-room. Marble was a conspicuous feature of the dining-saloon and the swimming-pool was decorated in green and black marble and fitted with under-water lighting effects.'

Among Canadian Pacific's chief competitors were a number of American and Japanese lines, several of which, like Canadian Pacific, benefited after the First World War from war surplus, including ex-German vessels. Conspicuous in the Pacific trade were the American Dollar Line, with its *Presidents* fleet, and the Matson Line. The latter, although noted for a round-the-world service, was content at one stage to put its *pièce de résistance*, the 17,000-ton liner *Malolo*, on the San Francisco–Honolulu run to serve the new Pacific playground for the Hollywood film colony. In 1927, when she appeared, this vessel was said to be the finest liner built hitherto in the United States: she had a speed of 22 knots and luxurious accommodation devoted almost entirely to first-class passengers.

The Canadian-Pacific liner *Empress of Australia*, seen here off Southampton in 1928, was one of the ships engaged in the trans-Pacific service between America and the Far East.

The facilities on board *Malolo* offered 'a perfection in detail that is seldom matched ... The public rooms which occupy the whole of one deck are so generous in size that one would think they belonged to a ship of much greater size ... The dining saloon is an exquisite room distinguished by the painting of Lionel Waldon and decorated in white and gold; it offers a feast to the eye as well as to the appetite. The beautiful lounge decorated in gold and orchid with ebony black columns rising as if by illusion out of a deep carpet of restful blue. The veranda café is impressive in antique oak, with a smart cocktail bar nearby, the smoking room is also of oak with a restful atmosphere, there is also an attractive blue and gold writing room and a library of treasured volumes. The Pompeiian swimming pool is a triumph of gorgeous hues ... Super luxury suites are also provided complete with private baths and lavatories ...' and so on.

The services into the Pacific through the Panama Canal were predominantly British, with Shaw Savill and New Zealand Shipping in the lead. The latter was known in the 1930s for its trio of sturdy comfortable motorships *Rangitani*, *Rangitata* and *Rangitiki*, each of just under 17,000 tons, with space for cargo as well as passengers. When these companies were hit by the Depression they went smartly into the cruising business, round-trips half across the world, from Britain to New Zealand and back, being found to be marketable commodities in winter. A typical tour comprised a hundred-day trip for an all-in fare there and back of £112; this included a month's stay in New Zealand, using the ship as a hotel, with calls en route at Pacific and West Indian islands.

Some of the best available ships were soon adapted to suit this traffic, including the provision in some cases of one (tourist) class in place of the previous two or three classes; and, despite the hard times, the early thirties marked the start of a widespread cruising 'boom' involving numerous shipping companies. In 1932, in liners operating from British ports alone, over one hundred thousand Britons went to sea for their holidays. Cruises ranged from three days to three weeks, the most popular period being a fortnight during which, besides covering up to four thousand miles in deep water, places could be visited as far afield as Scandinavia, the Atlantic islands and the western half of the Mediterranean.

But the real attraction was the excitement of life on board a large passenger ship at a grim, uncertain time when such a dazzling if rather vaguely comprehended prize seemed beyond the reach of the landlubber in the street – by today's standards, a rather stay-at-home creature! 'At first, everything seemed strange, different and also romantic – from the gaily-decorated dining-saloon with the most tempting dishes set out on a centre table to the elegant lounge and library and the warm, cosy smoking-room – rooms that seemed to have the whiff of adventure

Ocean travel was for masochists as well as sybarites: not a medieval torture chamber but a gymnasium on board an early ocean liner.

How to justify the daily over-eating rituals by primitive deck games
and exercises.

Left: If you were young and trim and refused the seventh and eighth courses at lunch, the odd drink between meals could surely do no harm.

and of distant lands about them . . . Then there were the decks, with their deck tennis-courts and other sports arenas, a luscious-looking swimming-pool . . . This is the life, you thought – and when you looked over the rail of the boat-deck at the quay below before the ship sailed, you felt dizzy at the height – but later on at sea, with the water foaming past, the dizziness had gone and in its place was a kind of fascination . . .'

The first liners purpose-built for cruising had appeared in 1927, the ancestor of them all being the 5,000-ton Norwegian *Stella Polaris*. 'Built like a yacht, with white hull and clipper stem, she was luxuriously fitted for some 200 passengers . . . and was mainly employed in cruising to the fiords and the Baltic.' One of the first liners to be converted permanently into a cruising ship was the equally famous British *Arandora Star*. This 13,000-ton vessel, withdrawn by Blue Star Line from the South American run, became the most luxurious cruising liner afloat. Designed originally to carry large quantities of (dead!) meat, some of her refrigerated holds became (live!) passenger accommodation, the promenade decks being extended and new public rooms created, including a ball-room and a garden lounge; and besides an open-air swimming pool, there was a sports deck measuring eighty feet by sixty feet.

Arandora Star, a South Atlantic meat-carrying liner in its early days, became after conversion one of the best-known and most luxurious cruising ships of the 1930s.

The new *Mauretania*, a stylish, confident successor to the Grand Old Lady of the Atlantic, enters dock at Southampton in 1939, on the eve of the Second World War.

Fond farewells in Bermudan sunshine as the British liner *Queen of Bermuda* sets forth on one of its regular festive voyages between that island and New York.

The Americans, seizing on this newest globe-trotting facility, were among the earlier and most eager cruise customers. Some of the beginnings were, however, fairly modest in price and duration. During the worst years of the Depression, Cunard employed some of its most splendid liners, between transatlantic voyages, on weekend cruises from New York. 'Never had such a novelty been afforded at so low a price. For four days, one could laze about the great decks of one of the most famous liners in the world and enjoy all the luxury usually reserved for millionaires, statesmen, business magnates and film stars.' All this, including a stop at Bermuda or Nassau, was obtained for a mere $50: within a few days of the first announcement, the first six cruises were fully booked.

Of course, one of the attractions during the period of

Prohibition in the United States was the chance to swallow a few drinks once these well-stocked British ships had left American territorial waters. For a time, this amenity was a prime attraction on a neat, compact, regular service which, for enterprise based on shrewd market assessment, deserves a special prize. This was the *Furness Withy* express service linking New York with the British possession of Bermuda. At its busiest season two sailings a week were available, these being provided from the early 1930s by the twins *Monarch of Bermuda* and *Queen of Bermuda*. In the former 'every state-room had a bathroom or a shower attached and the accommodation was on a most lavish scale, special attention being paid to keeping a large amount of deck space clear for out-door exercise. There were two swimming pools, indoor and outdoor, three

veranda cafés and extensive dancing space ... The *Monarch* was a magnificent and powerful vessel to look at, with her three well-raked red and black funnels, two masts and massive slate grey hull. She could carry 830 first-class passengers and some 30 in the second class.' The *Queen* was similar but slightly faster, managing New York to Bermuda in less than thirty-six hours.

These fine vessels, known as the 'millionaire ships', sailed from New York late in the evening to provide arrival in the sunlit harbour of Bermuda shortly after breakfast two mornings later. Having disembarked, the passengers would grope their hung-over way a few hundred yards to one of the lavish resort hotels in their lush settings overlooking the anchorage. There, within arm's length of the plentiful bars, would be a chance to swim, play golf, sightsee, and eat or dance in the open air, before embarking three or four days later for the return run to New York. The consumption of alcohol was stupendous, continuous, deliberate and single-minded: and, of course, highly profitable to all concerned. But then, no more enticing format for a drinking spree for parched people has ever been devised!

The cruising liner created its own tastes and fashions. Sunbathing gear and swim suits for cruise passengers are on show (left) at Selfridge's, London, in 1936, though the moment of truth at sea, where sturdier clothes may not come amiss, is perhaps better depicted in the shipboard scene (below).

ORIENT·PACIFIC LINE

LONDON AND AVSTRALIA
HEAD OFFICE · FENCHVRCH AVENVE · LONDON · E·C
WEST END OFFICE · 28 COCKSPVR STREET · S·W

Above: A typical poster conveying a Middle Eastern flavour at a time when competition by the many users of the Suez Canal for Orient-bound passengers was at its height.

Right: Overland passengers on the long Cape to Cairo haul in the 1930s enjoyed the interludes between rail travel of passages by river steamer: tea, English-style, on the River Nile.

Above: Nonchalant elegance on an exotic Monte Carlo terrace during a moment ashore from the cruise liner anchored in the bay: a 1932 picture *pour encourager les autres*.

Left: Whether meant for pain or for pleasure, it surely costs a lot! A lady passenger takes a Turkish bath in *Berengaria*'s forbiddingly elaborate health centre in 1923.

4 RAIL TRAVEL ACROSS THE WORLD

The famous all-Pullman *Golden Arrow* London–Paris service.

The British portion of the *Golden Arrow* towards the end of its steam-hauled days makes haste for Dover.

In 1933 Cole Porter, who had a highly developed sense of style, was in Europe with his wife Linda. 'At Gare de l'Est ... Linda was standing there, her English maid behind her. All Linda's bags matched. Cole was standing there. All his bags matched too. His valet stood behind him ... When the Porters' party got on the train, there were numerous bedrooms reserved: one for Linda, one for Cole, one for Brent, as well as a sitting room, and assorted sleeping and work rooms for the servants.'

For those who had the money this, as George Eells tells us, is the way it was. For the connoisseur, and no doubt Cole Porter was among them, the epitome of international luxury travel by rail in Europe between the world wars was, perhaps, the London–Paris *Golden Arrow* service. This Pullman train, introduced in 1926, was in fact two trains: the one on the English side of the Channel and the other on the French, the two connecting smartly at Dover and Calais respectively with a fast, specially appointed packet plying between the rail-heads.

The present author, who used this train several times in the 1950s, when its style and amenities were well up to pre-war standard, recalled in an article published in the *Geographical Magazine* in 1964: 'A journey by this famous Pullman express is one of the world's great experiences, yet it is there for the taking every morning of the year from Victoria Station. There is an ageless quality about this train. The atmosphere remains genteel, the farewells leisurely ... The gleaming gold and brown livery of the train illuminates the screened-off murk of Platform 8. At the doorway of your coach a white-jacketed steward awaits you; inside in plush, ornate surroundings the early arrivals relax in their armchairs. Coffee, brandy and smoked salmon sandwiches are in the offing.' And in his book, *Independent Traveller*, he recounts: 'Here you are deliberately giving up seven hours of your day to savour one of life's rare pleasures. This is an occasion, not just a journey; haute cuisine on wheels, not just a couple of jaded meals; impeccable service, not just some weary steward's stint; a daily example of brilliant, effortless rail-sea-rail organisation.'

In the heyday of this service, the northbound run started at noon from Platform 1 of the Gare du Nord. The placard at the entrance gate read: '*Départ 12ʰ00. Golden Arrow Flèche D'or. Train de Luxe. Calais Mme et l'Angleterre*. The French train comprised brown and cream Pullman cars at the rear and blue *wagons lits* at the front, the latter having

The French portion of the *Golden Arrow* at Calais on its inaugural run in 1936, draws up beside the connecting packet to off-load its passengers.

been worked around the Ceinture loop from the Gare de Lyon, after arrival there as part of the *Blue Train* from the French Riviera or the *Rome Express* from Italy and Switzerland.

In the leading Pullman car 'a faint whiff of Chef Legrand's handiwork escapes from the crowded, coal-fired galley'; and with just over three hours before arrival at Calais there is time to do justice to the bill of fare, time 'for the *aperitif, hors-d'oeuvres, sole meunière, côte de veau portugaise, petits pois*, camembert, a half-bottle of *rosé*, coffee, a liqueur – and, deservedly, a short nap!'

Then, revived or, given ill-luck with the weather, relieved by the Channel crossing, the train waiting at Dover would be entered with renewed appetite for a cosy English tea including scones, buttered toast with jam and cream, currant cake, pastries and an individual pot of the consoling nectar. On the platform at Victoria, the last lap completed, porters, customs officers and a row of taxis would await the passenger's convenience; and, in a few minutes, he would be snugly ensconced in his West End hotel with a bath, change of clothes, cocktails and, assuming that he was now, once more, a little peckish, a fine five-course dinner in prospect.

The originator of deluxe travel by rail was the American, George Pullman, who in the 1860s introduced the first purpose-built sleeping cars, convertible by day into parlours, saloons or dining cars. Other countries followed suit with sleeping cars of their own making but the Pullman day car was transplanted more or less exactly from North America into several European railway systems; and its inventor's name remained associated with this refined form of travel until the species became extinct in the 1960s.

By the 1870s the way was clear for the organization of long-distance journeys though, as explained in Chapter 1, a number of political and technical problems prevented progress. These gave the Belgian, Georges Nagelmackers, his opportunity and the result of his initiatives were the formation of the renowned *Compagnie Internationale des Wagons-lits et des Grands Express Européens*. The early coaches had only four wheels. A washroom in the centre of each car connected with three compartments which were sitting-rooms by day and bedrooms at night.

In 1881 Nagelmackers ordered his first restaurant cars. These had seats for twelve customers, gas lighting, coal-fired kitchens and, always, a *cuisine soignée*. These developments led in 1883 to the inaugural run of the *Orient*

Express which, as Bryan Morgan wrote in *The Great Trains*, 'after the first flurry of journalistic attention ... settled down to the transporting of diplomats and exporters, of health-seekers, and above all ... of grand-tourists'. This train ran from Paris to Bucharest, whence the journey to Constantinople was continued by boat, the whole trip taking eighty hours. This time was soon reduced to seventy hours with the completion of a through railway-line and, from 1894, a connection from London via Ostend, the *Ostend–Vienna Express*, brought the facility within easier reach of its British clients.

From its earliest days the *Orient Express* excited world-wide interest. Its pioneering version, according to the Frenchman, Edmond About, provided a salon for the ladies, a smoking-room for the gentlemen and a refrigeration system which 'enabled passengers to enjoy butter from Normandy throughout the journey'. The chefs offered traditional dishes of the countries through which the express travelled: no mean feat considering that, in its heyday, the train crossed twelve frontiers. By the end of the nineteenth century, as J P Pearson has recorded, the woodwork in the sleeping cars of the *Orient Express* was 'dark brown, with a dark yellow leather, which had a gilt figuring in the corner as relief. Berths and carpet matched one another in a dark blue material with a greenish-white pattern, and the ceiling was painted with a blue, flowered cornice and a large "star" design on a whitish-blue ground'; while in the smoking-room there were 'arm-chairs in red plush, a red-figured carpet and diamond-shaped panels in brown and green on the side walls and ceiling'.

As the present author wrote in *The Great Trains*, many variations and offshoots of the original *Orient Express* came into being over the years, among them the *Simplon* (formerly *Simplon–Orient*) *Express*, the *Arlberg* (formerly *Arlberg–Orient*) *Express*, the *Direct–Orient Express* and, more recently, the *Tauern–Orient Express*.

In the 1930s the route of the *Orient Express* itself was from Calais (from which through cars were by now also available) and Paris through Germany, Austria, Czechoslovakia, Hungary and Rumania, the train terminating, as before, at Bucharest. But, as we learn in *Railway Wonders of the World*, there was now also 'the closely-associated *Simplon–Orient Express* which takes its way farther south, through Switzerland, Italy and Yugoslavia' and thence through Bulgaria to Istanbul (formerly Constantinople), the two trains going their separate ways after Budapest. A journey by these trains 'is, to a dull person, merely a means of getting across Europe. To those with imagination ... it is a source of fascinating instruction ... There is no tedium on a long railway journey, least of all on one which takes you through the most important countries in Europe ... One can contrast the fine modern railway systems and rolling-stock of

Boat trains serving ocean liners were once a familiar part of the railway scene. Sir Thomas Lipton leaves London for New York in 1929 in pursuit of the elusive America Cup.

France and Germany with very different things in the Balkans. One can look out of the beautifully appointed sleeping compartment ... into the bare wooden compartment of some unfamiliar local train, where half-Eastern looking peasants are smoking long gilt pipes over queer bundles of farm produce, stacked in the middle of the floor ... The train has an opulent air; the cars travel with little vibration, the equipment is extraordinarily comfortable and clean ... The conductor of our car has taken care of our passports and tickets, so we will not be disturbed in the night ...'

At the turn of the century, the growing Nagelmackers' empire was crowned with his *Trans-Siberian International Express*, providing the first overland service between Western Europe and the Far East. According to Paul Price, 'here was a train more luxurious even than anything Nagelmackers had created before. There was a library, with books in English, French, German and Russian; a music room with a full-sized grand piano; a hair-dressing salon; a gymnasium, and even a chapel. The route took the travellers through Siberia ... to Peking on what one early traveller called "an ambulant palace of luxury".'

Several decades later, Peter Fleming wrote: 'There is a great deal to be said against trains, but it will not be said by me. I like the Trans-Siberian Railway ... You wake up in the morning ... Your berth is comfortable. There is no need to get up, and no incentive either. You have nothing to look forward to, nothing to avoid. No assets, no liabilities ... So, in the end, you get up, washing perfunctorily in the little dark confessional which you share with the next compartment ... Then, grasping your private pot of marmalade, you lurch along to the dining car ... (which) is almost certainly stuffy, but you have ceased to notice this. The windows are always shut, either because the weather is cold, or because it is warm and dry and therefore dusty ...

'After that you wander back to your compartment. The *provodnik* has transformed your bed into a seat ... You sit down and read. You read and read and read. There are no distractions, no interruptions, no temptations to get up and do something else; there is nothing else to do. You read as you have never read before ... At last evening comes. The sun is setting somewhere far back along the road that you have travelled. A slanting light always lends intimacy to a landscape, and this Siberia, flecked darkly by the

But for the Second World War, the dream of a Cape to Cairo through-railway route, with connections right across Europe to the Arctic, would long since have become a reality. The map (right) portrays some of the gaps and problems as the dream took shape; while the inviting picture (left) shows the Cairo terminus of the proposed service.

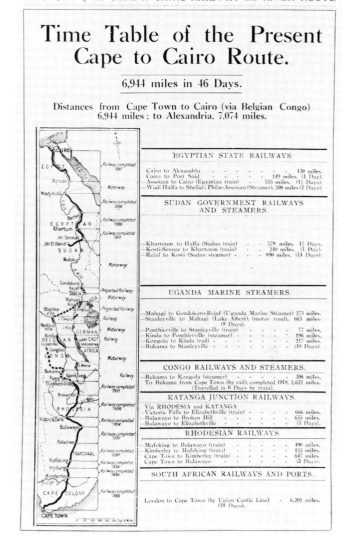

Time Table of the Present Cape to Cairo Route.

6,944 miles in 46 Days.

Distances from Cape Town to Cairo (via Belgian Congo) 6,944 miles; to Alexandria, 7,074 miles.

EGYPTIAN STATE RAILWAYS.

Cairo to Alexandria	- - - -	130 miles.
Cairo to Port Said	- -	149 miles. (1 Day).
Assouan to Cairo (Egyptian train)	-	555 miles. (1 Day).
Wadi Halfa to Shellal; Philæ-Assouan (Steamer), 208 miles (2 Days).		

SUDAN GOVERNMENT RAILWAYS AND STEAMERS.

Khartoum to Halfa (Sudan train)	-	579 miles. 1½ Days.
Kosti-Sennar to Khartoum (train)	-	240 miles. (1 Day).
Rejaf to Kosti (Sudan steamer) - -	-	890 miles. (14 Days).

UGANDA MARINE STEAMERS.

Mahagi to Gondokoro-Rejaf (Uganda Marine Steamer) 273 miles.		
Stanleyville to Mahagi (Lake Albert), (motor road), 683 miles. (8 Days).		
Ponthierville to Stanleyville (train)	-	77 miles.
Kindu to Ponthierville (steamer)	- -	196 miles.
Kongola to Kindu (rail)	- - -	217 miles.
Bukama to Stanleyville - - -	-	(10 Days).

CONGO RAILWAYS AND STEAMERS.

Bukama to Kongola (steamer)	- - -	398 miles.
To Bukama from Cape Town (by rail), completed 1918, 2,632 miles. (Travelled in 6 Days by train).		

KATANGA JUNCTION RAILWAYS.

Via RHODESIA and KATANGA		
Victoria Falls to Elizabethville (train)	- -	666 miles.
Bulawayo to Broken Hill	- - -	655 miles.
Bulawayo to Elizabethville	-	(3 Days).

RHODESIAN RAILWAYS.

Mafeking to Bulawayo (train)	- -	490 miles.
Kimberley to Mafeking (train)	- -	123 miles.
Cape Town to Kimberley (train)	- -	647 miles.
Cape Town to Bulawayo	-	(3 Days).

SOUTH AFRICAN RAILWAYS AND PORTS.

London to Cape Town (by Union Castle Line)	-	6,201 miles. (18 Days).

tapering shadows of trees, seems a place at once more friendly and more mysterious than the naked non-committal flats of noon.'

Many of the famous trains at the turn of the century illustrate clearly the dictates of fashion. The Côte d'Azur, a one-time playground for the rich and rare thanks to the lead given by Queen Victoria and her son Edward, was served at the peak of its development by trains with these tell-tale names: *Calais–Mediterranean* (later *Blue Train*), *St Petersburg–Vienna–Nice*, *Riviera* (from Berlin and Amsterdam), *Rome–Florence–Cannes*, and for Parisians, the *Nice Express*. No wonder there survives even today, in the smart Cimiez quarter of Nice, a statue of Queen Victoria. In *The Great Trains* we read that 'This powerful woman, through her annual presence in that city in the late 1890s, bestowed upon the area the kind of accolade which made it a mecca of lesser royalties and their entourages in the *Belle Epoque*. Her son Edward helped too, for before becoming obsessed by Biarritz and the Côte Basque, he favoured Cannes while regarding the Riviera in general as "un pays de bonne compagnie où tout le monde se retrouve, comme dans une *garden-party*".'

This coast is fortunate, indeed, in never having lost its appeal. 'After the First World War, for example, the Americans adopted it: due largely to their influence . . . it became a summer as well as a winter resort by the simple expedient of opening its ample facilities all the year round', access to it being still chiefly by train. This trend towards a summer season 'suited well the new European "whoopee"-makers of the twenties – most of whom, being obliged to work for their living, vacationed when the days were hot enough to frolic quietly by the sea and the nights warm enough for more zestful fun and games beneath the stars.'

This was the era in Europe of the glamorous Pullman expresses 'with their individual armchairs at softly-lit tables for two, of "grand-hotel" décor and of impeccable service by hand-picked stewards'. For the British, the *Golden Arrow* with its attached through sleeping-cars offered one way of getting to the Mediterranean; this famous train was challenged, from 1929, by the equally golden *Côte d'Azur Rapide*. The tradition of luxury on this route continues to this day. The *Blue Train* still runs, though no longer with through cars from Calais, the British now being served by a train called the *Flandre–Riviera*

A news picture of 1876 eloquently depicts the ordeal of hungry passengers in an overcrowded station buffet as their train waits impatiently to resume its journey.

Express, which includes through sleeping and couchette cars from Calais. And there is the famous *Mistral*, from Paris to Nice in nine hours, 'the last word in European opulence, all first class with restaurant cars, bar, hairdressing salon, boutique, bookshop and secretarial services, but with three seats across the carriage instead of the former Pullman's two'.

As a glance at rail timetables in the early twentieth century makes clear, the British were the most influential customers for the European expresses. Even a decade or two ago, *Cook's Continental Timetable* (since renamed the *Thomas Cook International Timetable*) showed a mass of routes, served by famous expresses, radiating across Europe like the spokes of a wheel, from the concentrated hub of the ports facing England. In its palmy days this traffic included 'special' trains, such as the *Malle des Indes*, serving the Raj. This train resulted from an initiative by the French in 1855; it carried mails overland to Marseilles to be loaded there into Orient-bound P & O ships, thus saving several days on the journey to India and beyond. From 1869, the train's route was extended to Brindisi and, with the connecting liners calling there, even more time was saved. Passenger travel began in 1880, the train at that time needing forty-eight hours for its journey across Europe.

In 1890 the train was divided into two: the *Peninsular Express* and, on the more fashionable route to Marseilles, the *Bombay Express*. Before long the latter became the sole connecting link, and survived until 1939. It offered a fine facility 'for Britons and their ladies privileged to go about imperial business in "posh" style: with an afternoon departure from London after a leisurely lunch in club or hotel the passengers reached Calais in time to join a sleeping-and-restaurant car express which conveyed them swiftly through the night to provide an after-breakfast arrival at Marseilles', where their ship awaited them.

Other distinguished trains of that period, well known to the European traveller, and not least the British, included the *Rheingold* (which continues today), the *Londres–Vichy* and the *Calais–Brussels* Pullmans and, from 1936, the *Night Ferry*. The latter (another survivor), with its through sleeping-cars conveyed by ship across the Channel, was Britain's only truly 'international' train. There were also the *Nord*, which ran from Paris and Ostend through Berlin to St Petersburg, providing a connection with the *Trans-Siberian* (and today goes instead through Hamburg to Copenhagen with connections there for Stockholm); and its famous counterpart, the *Sud*.

In its best days the *Sud*, originating from Paris, provided connections at Lisbon with ocean liners bound for South Africa and South America and at Algeciras with Orient-bound ships waiting in Gibraltar Bay. The Spanish portion of this train, routed via Madrid, provided connections at Algeciras also with the ferry to Tangier

Above: The immense yet
delicately-wrought pillared
lounge of the *Normandie* which,
with the adjacent smoking room,
could be merged into one
enormous salon; and (below) this
fantastic liner's first-class
restaurant, 'a *tour de force* of
tinted glass . . . longer than the
famed Hall of Mirrors at
Versailles'.

Opposite above: In 1936 the legendary *Queen Mary*, a magnificent 80,000-ton monster—although not to everyone's taste in interior design—joined the North Atlantic throng. A view of this great liner's cabin-class lounge.

Opposite below: In the 1930s the Americans, reluctant to enter the truly big transatlantic league, fielded the relatively modest but highly successful *Manhattan* and *Washington*. The latter alongside at Florida in 1935.

which, in turn, connected with the Moroccan rail service to Casablanca. This express, like other long-distance trains of the past, is no longer what it was, though, as the present author wrote recently in *The Great Trains*: 'Even today, the Spanish, Portuguese and Moroccan timetables announce this train with a kind of faded flourish. Its connections with Africa are given ... but the process is not speedy, allowing a day in Madrid ... Edward VII would no longer use it to Biarritz, nor Alphonso XIII to San Sebastian. Yet, until quite recently, the French portion of this train carried only first-class passengers, some in Pullman splendour; these latter were served from a separate kitchen with meals superior even to those of the ordinary dining car.

'Today the *Sud* no longer rates a supplement for speed or merit, the Pullman is no more, and the shared dining car lazily serves the same menu at lunch and dinner.'

However, at Irun, as part of the Portuguese portion, 'in its distinctive blue livery is the train's only sleeping car, bearing ornately along its length the title *Compania Internacional de Coches-Camas*, and below this the words *Sud Express: Paris–Lisboa*'; and, as we have always been led to expect where European international sleeping cars are concerned, 'through the dimly-lit windows one glimpses in one sleeping-compartment a slender grey-haired man with a *hidalgo*'s aquiline nose and, in another and in the act of closing her door for the night, what legend would have one believe to be the adornment of all overnight expresses in Europe – a blonde, cool, full-bosomed and alluring'.

Of the trains travelling further afield, of those penetrating beyond the outer rim of Europe, the most enterprising and, perhaps, exciting was the *Taurus Express*, an extension into the Middle East of the *Orient* fraternity. This train, introduced in 1930, started its journey at Haydarpasa, the other side of the Bosphorus from Istanbul, and, after crossing the mountains of Turkey, entered Syria. At Aleppo it divided, one portion

Train passengers in most civilized countries were lunching in style, thanks to George Pullman's influence, even before the *Orient Express* made its début in the 1880s.

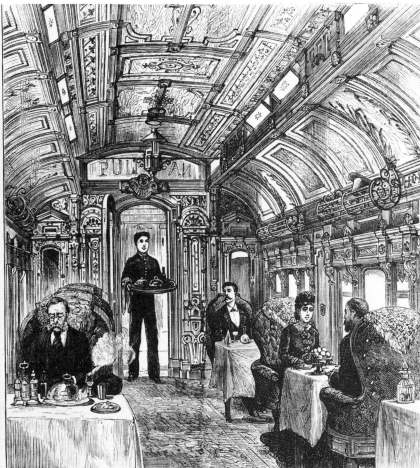

The tables-for-two arrangement of Pullman day cars survived in Europe until the end of that species a decade ago.

Right: Among the comforts for passengers at the turn of the century were footwarmers loaded from the platform at the start of the journey and renewed as necessary en route.

proceeding towards Beirut and the other to Baghdad, this second portion including a through sleeping-car for the whole fifty-hour journey from Haydarpasa.

Passengers for the Lebanon and beyond were conveyed by a special motorcoach via Beirut to Haifa, the latter being eleven hours' journey from Aleppo. At Haifa a through express-train, with sleeping and dining cars, awaited the on-going passenger; the train, having crossed the Suez Canal by swing-bridge, terminated at Cairo. Using the *Orient Express*, the *Taurus Express* and the subsequent conveyances via Haifa, Cairo was brought within seven days' travel of London. Apart from short breaks, by Nile river steamer or, further on, by motorbus, the Cape to Cairo through-railway dream was by now almost a reality; and, but for the intervention of the Second World War, would long since have made possible a continuous journey by train from within the Arctic Circle to Cape Town.

The British were, of course, pioneer builders and operators as well as patrons of railways. In their own country there has long existed one of the densest railway systems in the world, worked by numerous famous expresses. Of these the best known is the *Flying Scotsman* which, since 1862 has left King's Cross for Edinburgh daily at 10.00 hours. In the 1930s the train's equipment boasted, besides an ornate restaurant car, a ladies' retiring-room and a hairdressing

salon. However, as Bryan Morgan records: 'The latter seems to have been under-used, since in 1938 the *coiffeur* was replaced with a mere ladies-maid: but throughout the thirties male passengers could pass the time whilst their women-folk were being titivated by not merely reading bulletins assembled from news received on the train's wireless but studying radio-photographs of – for instance – the finish of the Derby.'

Railway Wonders of the World bids us, in the mid-1930s, to 'look now at the *Flying Scotsman* as it stands at No. 10 platform at King's Cross. Next to the engine comes a through composite coach ... for Perth. After that there is the Glasgow portion' and then 'a varying number of third-class compartment coaches ... all of the latest and most comfortable type, with arm-rests dividing up the seats into three places on each side. Large toilet compartments are placed on these cars, and a supply of hot water can be obtained both winter and summer ... Down the side of the corridor of the next coach there are illuminated projecting signs, similar to those in the corridor of an hotel. The first door on the left is labelled "Hairdressing Saloon", which caters for both men and women. Next to this is a "Ladies' Retiring Room", and then ... the "Cocktail Bar". This is a delightfully-furnished room with ultra-modern decorations in green and silver, and the pleasantest of haunts in which to pass half an hour on the journey. Beyond the bar are the

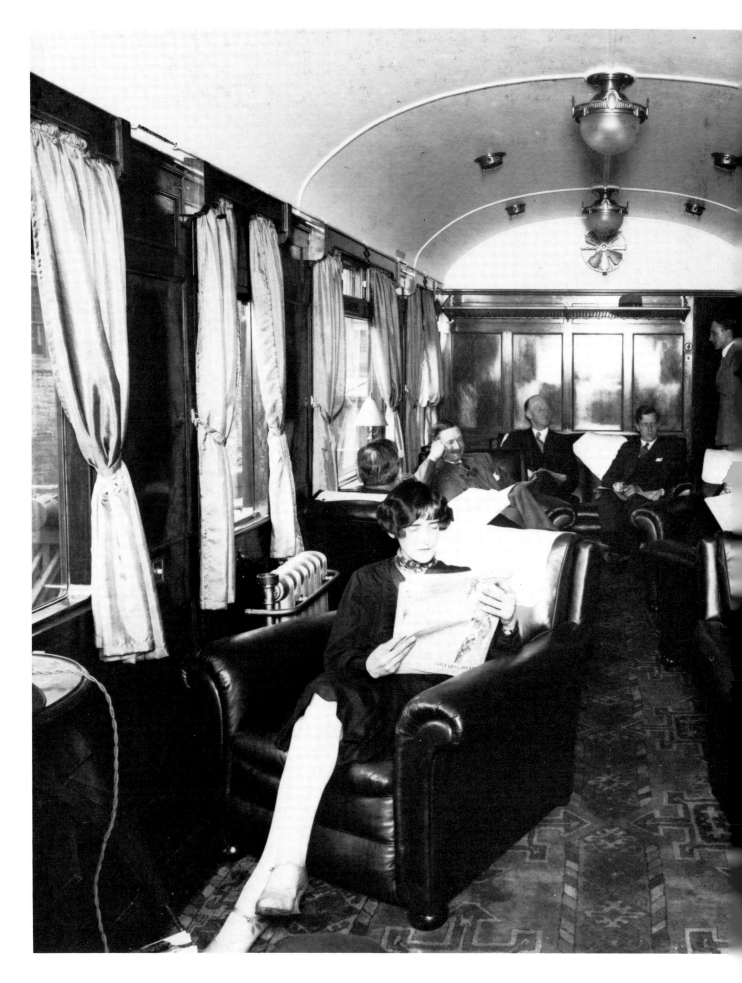

In the early 1930s, British express trains were second to none in the provision of luxurious amenities, including services for businessmen. (Left) shows a lounge car of the *Royal Scot* London to Glasgow service, while (above) depicts a stenographer on the London to Newcastle express keeping her distance from a hesitant tycoon.

Was any railway vehicle ever quite as long and broad? This romanticized view of an early Pullman dining car gains much from a bit of artist's licence.

restaurant cars ... The first-class restaurant car on the *Flying Scotsman* is a luxurious conveyance, furnished and decorated throughout in the Louis XVI period style, with concealed lighting. So is the first-class compartment coach immediately following it ... The name "*The Flying Scotsman*" is carried on the roof of each coach, on both sides; ... on the front of the engine smoke-box; and ... on the rear end of the last coach.'

This superior service, and that offered on the impressive rival, the *Royal Scot*, star of the Euston to Glasgow route, were largely the outcome of the great speed contest known as the Race to the North. In essence, according to *Steam Trains*, the competition was 'between the groups of companies operating the east coast and west coast routes from London to Scotland. In 1885 the fastest train on the west coast route ... was completing the journey from London to Edinburgh in 10 hours. On the east coast route, the *Flying Scotsman* was doing the journey in only 9 hours ... The west coast route began to lose passengers so a 9-hour service was introduced. The east coast promptly

responded with an 8½-hour journey' upon which 'the east coast introduced a service which took 30 minutes less. Six days later the west coast achieved 8 hours' but finally, the companies agreed to apply a limit of just over 8 hours. Today, the diesel-powered high-speed train version of the *Flying Scotsman* manages King's Cross–Edinburgh in a few minutes under five hours, while the electric loco-hauled counterpart covers the Euston–Glasgow run in five hours precisely.

Two other internationally famous British trains are the *Cornish Riviera* and (no longer with us, alas) the *Brighton Belle*. The former, connecting Paddington, through Exeter and Plymouth, with Cornwall made its bow in the early years of the century when, among other useful facilities, came 'the provision of a valet to clean the gentlemen's boots and of a maid dressed in nurse's uniform to "constantly patrol the train" and "especially watch over ladies travelling without an escort" (both these for third-class passengers, since the thirty-six first-class travellers were expected to have their own servants)'.

The contemporary *Cornish Riviera*, a speeded-up version of its forebears, is still one of Britain's most romantic holiday expresses, working a route unrivalled for its variety of scenery. The *Brighton Belle*, as its name implies, covered

Even the lowest class of passenger was well catered for in British trains in the 1930s. (Below) shows an early self-service buffet car on a short-distance inter-city express; and (above) third-class passengers enjoy red-carpet treatment aboard the London to Edinburgh *Flying Scotsman*.

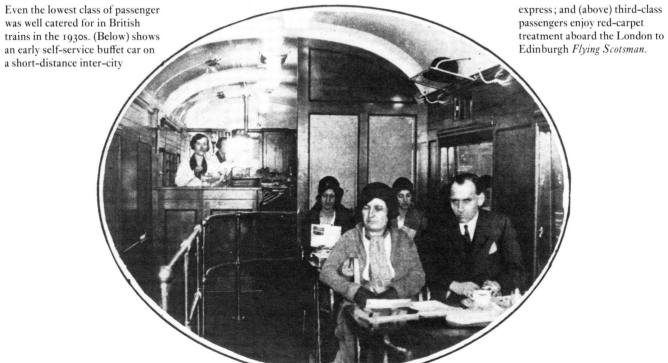

in one hour the relatively short distance separating London and Brighton. This was an all-Pullman train, originally steam-hauled and, in its later days, an electrically-driven multiple-unit train. With a service twice a day in each direction, and a crew adept at fast delivery of meals and refreshments, it provided a lush, plush and lively link between the bright lights of London's West End and the saucy glamour of the capital's nearest and most beautiful seaside resort. In its heyday the *Brighton Belle* carried a higher proportion than any other train of well-known theatre and film stars, socialites and businessmen, honeymoon couples and 'dirty' weekenders, cardsharpers and pimps, and other personalities of equal note. Today, if they travel that route (and fewer do, there being no trains of special distinction), they must needs go by car; and that, of course, is the story of the life (and death) of all the short-to-middle distance luxury trains.

Many of the early railway networks in far-off countries, from South America across Africa to India and the Far East, also owed their origins to the British engineer. The railways of India have always had a special appeal for train enthusiasts. David Tennant, writing in *The Great Trains*, tells us that 'when the first railway in India opened between Bombay and Thana on 16 April, 1853, it did so amidst "a loud applause of a vast multitude and the salute of 21 guns" in the presence of 400 distinguished guests ... Few countries in the world presented such hazardous conditions for railway construction', yet, by the end of the nineteenth century, due largely to pressures by the military, the total railway mileage in India exceeded 40,000. Luxury, for those who could afford it, has always been an Indian keynote. The Frenchman, Louis Rousselet, writing in 1865 about a five-day train journey from Calcutta, slept 'on a comfortable little bed, walking up and down in my carriage during the day ... These carriages contained only two compartments in each of which there is but a single seat, the movable back of which takes off, and being fastened by leather straps forms a sort of couch of the same description as the beds in ship's cabins. On the opposite side of the carriage are two closets – one for the toilet and the other the convenience ... At stations provided with buffets I found a servant who, when he had taken the orders for my meal, telegraphed it to the next station where my breakfast or dinner awaited my arrival'.

Thomas Cook, the leading exponent of nineteenth-century travel, wrote about an Indian train in 1873: 'For my party a saloon carriage with sleeping berths, baths and closets was allotted and this we kept for three weeks ... The Indian sleeping carriages are a modification of the American system and although they do not in India furnish bedding and attendance, there is no extra charge for the carriage and it was cheaper to buy stuffed bed-quilts and pillows than to pay three dollars a night for the American accommodation.'

After George VI came to the throne in 1937, the *Coronation Scot*, with its streamlined locomotive, became the star train on Britain's important London to Glasgow route.

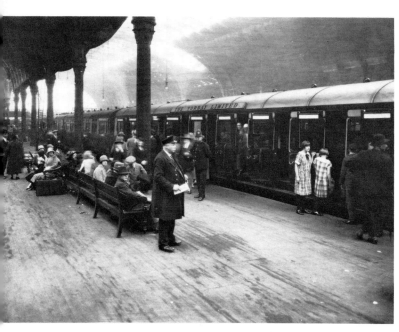

To many Londoners, Paddington Station, one of the capital's most distinguished rail termini, has long conjured up visions of sunlit seaside holidays in England's West Country. These 1920s views show two Great Western expresses, the *Cornish Riviera* (right) and *Torbay Limited* (above) preparing to leave.

In the 1930s, according to *Railway Wonders of the World*, the first-class passenger in India 'will occupy a compartment which is about 12ft. long and 8ft. wide, with accommodation for six persons by day and four by night. He will find two sofas running lengthwise, surmounted by two upper berths, which are let down at night for sleeping purposes. Each compartment will have a lavatory and bathroom, two or more electric fans, adequate lighting, including bed lamps, probably two armchairs, a small collapsible table and a chest of drawers ... and [he] will probably be accompanied by a native servant who travels in a special compartment at the end of the carriage ... There are, however, two things that militate against comfort. These are heat and dust, over neither of which, unfortunately, have the railway authorities any control'. On the question of heat, 'electric fans are of little avail' as 'they do nothing but blow hot streams of air upon the already overheated body. It is, however, possible to buy large blocks of ice which are placed in containers on the floor of the compartment, which do something to bring the temperature down.'

We have this reminiscence also from Raymonde Horner, a relation of the present author: 'Before World War Two there were many jokes about the "fishing fleet", the name given to the bevies of girls who went out to India at their own expense in search of husbands among the British soldiery stationed there. They were usually the relations or friends of married officers who, accompanied by their wives, could offer chaperoned hospitality. Most travelled from England by sea, arriving at the end of October in Bombay, to be met by an agent who would introduce the

Piles of heavy personal baggage were always a feature of stations and quaysides in the grand days of travel: a typical load at London's Victoria Station, awaiting cross-Channel shipment.

No service was too much trouble aboard the sleeping cars of British trains in the 1930s. In this scene an attendant of a Scottish express distributes hot-water bottles.

There were ample opportunities between the world wars for railway excursions for the adventurous: a transandine tourist train halts at an Argentinian station during its long haul over the mountains.

By the closing years of the nineteenth century American trains had acquired their own distinctively rugged look, as befitted the main carriers of a pioneering nation.

newcomer to her bearer or head servant. The bearer, a very superior Indian, whose status was obvious from his umbrella, would conduct his young lady to the train which would lay on a carriage complete with bed, lavatory, washbasin and table, her home for the two or three-day journey into the interior.

'The Bombay–Calcutta express was air-conditioned but on lesser trains in hot weather the only means of air-cooling was a block of ice brought in by the bearer at each station. The bearer would also lay a table and provide meals, the train stopping long enough for him to fetch and serve the food before withdrawing to his own inferior carriage. There were no corridors and the windows were shut against the dust and barred against dacoits. The steam trains were rather magnificent, even if they achieved only 25mph, and travellers remember vividly the dense mass of Indian bodies on the platform over which they had to tread when they wished to stretch their legs.'

The story of the early days of rail travel in North America is largely the story of the efforts to provide direct links from the Atlantic to the Pacific. By 1890, four routes across the United States of America and one across Canada were already in operation; most of the present rail network in both countries was complete; and American long-distance express trains were averaging 40mph or more.

But the taste for luxury and glamour is also an important part of the American story. And when it came to naming trains, no country was more inventive than the United

Opposite above: One of America's most famous expresses, the *Twentieth Century Limited*, promoted in the 1920s as 'The Greatest Train in the World', provided an overnight service linking New York with Chicago.

Opposite below: A British express train, with St Pancras Station and Hotel in the background, leaves London for the North. The routes to Scotland were long the scene of fierce competition for passengers.

THE NEW YORK CENTRAL.
"TWENTIETH CENTURY LIMITED."

By the closing years of the nineteenth century American trains had acquired their own distinctively rugged look as befitted the chief carriers of a pioneering nation.

Opposite: A *rapide* in a hurry thunders south towards France's Côte d'Azur, along the railway line patronized for years more than any other by Europe's richest and most distinguished pleasure-seeking travellers.

States where seven hundred were advertised in this way. Many of those have become world-famous: above all, perhaps, those vigorous competitors on the New York–Chicago run, the *Broadway Limited* and the *Twentieth Century Limited*. The latter, introduced in 1902, with specially built sleeping cars, set new standards in luxury; and in the 1920s, confident as ever, its operators were promoting it noisily as 'The Greatest Train in the World'.

The great rival, the *Broadway Limited*, still offered a fine experience in the years after the Second World War. The present author, recalling in *Independent Traveller* a journey made in the early 1960s, recorded how this train 'offers a lounge car with bar and a splendidly plush restaurant on wheels, complete with tail-coated maîtres d'hotel ... You can retire after dinner to your private sitting-room, thence into a proper bed for the night. In the morning, a refreshing shower; if you wish, willing hands will bring a full breakfast to your sitting-room; and under the door will

'It's all here!' This American eulogy of twentieth-century passenger travel by every means in all the elements shows how it seemed on the eve of the First World War.

Opposite: Benjamin Franklin heading west in grand style.

appear your private copy of the weather forecast, accompanied by arrival information, all specially printed on the way. Finally, as you approach your destination, you may complete your engagements for the day by telephoning from the train.'

Among the many transcontinental expresses in the 1930s (and there were five daily trains from Chicago to California alone) the *Santa Fé Chief* was, perhaps, the most famous, if only because it was much used by film stars travelling to and from Los Angeles. According to *Railway Wonders of the World*, 'the "Chief" is frankly intended for those people who want the best ... for men who demand the extra roaming space provided by the club cars and for women who love daintiness and immaculate surroundings'. In the air-conditioned club car 'expert barbering is also obtainable, and there is the luxury of a shower bath for men as well as women'.

Furthermore 'the first air-cooled diner ever used in the West was installed in the "Chief" ... Fine table linen, gleaming silver, harmonious decoration and immaculate daintiness everywhere serve to whet the appetite ...

The great days of American steam haulage: two 1941 views of express trains at speed. The *Morning Daylight* (left above) with fifteen cars, touching 80mph, in California; and the fourteen-car *Pacific Limited* (left below) heading west out of Denver.

Midway in the train and next to the diner is the special ten-section lounge car, with its luxurious settees and chairs and its tables with reading lamps . . . a pleasant meeting-place for friendships so often made on long-distance trains of this nature. Passing through the sleeping-cars you notice that sleeping sections, drawing-rooms and compartments are so well contrived that they may be booked by the suite; indeed the "Chief" is little less than a travelling hotel . . . At the rear of the train is the observation super-parlour car' and 'in this part of the train there is also a lounge reserved for the use of women passengers . . . A maid travels with a train to attend to the needs of the feminine travellers, a negro maid – as is the custom there – all shiny and clean, and ever ready to respond to the demands for service.'

In the 1920s and 1930s the variety of accommodation available in American trains was quite bewildering. Among the many forms of refreshment car were the Compartment Observation Car comprising lounge, three sleeping compartments with drawing-room, library and buffet service – in effect, a self-contained luxury apartment for both day and night use; the Club Compartment Car, with rather similar facilities but, sadly, without the library and special windows for viewing the scenery; the Solarium Lounge Car, with its observation room furnished with armchairs, separate smoking room, ladies' lounge, library, buffet service and shower baths; and a miscellany of more modest eating places such as the Observation Café Parlor Car, Buffet Parlor Car and Broiler Buffet.

The 'Standard' sleeping accommodation was not very inviting. Pairs of seats became berths, supplemented by an extra row of berths let down from the car's upper sides; the two rows of berths stretched the whole length of the carriage, with curtains for privacy on either side of the central gangway. The bashful passenger had to undress, most awkwardly, half-crouching on his berth behind the curtains. Each car offered a separate smoking-room, washrooms with several hand-basins, as well as lavatories. More attractive, for some, was the so-called Drawing Room, a self-contained compartment with a sofa berth and a private lavatory. Thus, a typical long-distance train offered a wide choice of day cars, parlour and coach cars, refreshment cars and sleeping cars. While some of the best features survive under the current Amtrack scheme, standardization has removed much of the variety.

In America, as elsewhere, speed was yet another part of the story. As Gérard Vuillet recounts: 'A complete change in the speed of American passenger trains took place in the decade from 1927 onwards. While previously the normal running speed of the best trains was in the region of 65mph, in 1937 a speed of 80mph on level track was current for standard heavy trains . . . As regards long-distance traffic, the diesel-hauled trans-continental trains operated between Chicago and the Pacific Coast were in a class apart, the two most outstanding services being the *City of San Francisco* covering the 2,261 miles between Chicago and San Francisco, in 39.75hr at 56.9mph, over the lines of the Chicago and North Western Railway, the Union Pacific and the Southern Pacific Railroads, and the *Super Chief* of the Atchison, Topeka and Santa Fé Railway which took the same time to cover 2,227 miles between Chicago and Los Angeles at 56mph. Both routes crossed extremely difficult territory through the two mountain ranges found between the central plains and the Pacific.'

In Europe the highest average speeds were to be found in Germany but, as the accompanying table shows, France, Italy and Britain were also in the big league:

Fastest trains on the eve of the Second World War

Country	Train	Run	Dis-tance	Time h m	Speed mph	No of stops	Power*
Germany	*Fliegende Kölner*	Berlin–Hamm	267.6	3 16	81.9	1	D
Germany	FD T 45	Berlin–Breslau	204.7	2 34	79.7	0	D
USA, Santa Fé	*Super Chief*	La Junta–Dodge City	202.4	2 35	78.3	0	DL
Germany	*Fliegende Hamburger*	Berlin–Hamburg	178.2	2 17	78.0	0	D
USA, Union Pacific	*City of Denver*	Julesbourg–Kearney	176.2	2 19	76.1	1	DL
USA, Milwaukee	*Hiawatha* (eastbound)	La Crosse–Watertown	150.7	1 59	76.0	2	DL
Germany	F D 24	Berlin–Hamburg	178.2	2 24	74.2	0	SL
France	8028	Nancy–Paris	219.1	3 00	73.0	0	P
Great Britain LNER	*The Coronation*	London–York	188.2	2 37	71.9	0	SL
USA, Milwaukee	*The Hiawatha* (westbound)	Chicago–La Crosse	281.6	4 00	70.4	3	SL
Great Britain, LNER	*The Silver Jubilee*	London–Darlington	232.8	3 18	70.4	0	SL
France	*Sud-Express* No 8	Bordeaux–Les Aubrais	286.5	4 06	69.9	3	EL
Italy	525 and 527	Milan–Florence	195.8	2 50	69.1	1	E
France	8	Lyons–Paris	317.7	4 39	68.4	2	P
Great Britain, LNER	*The West Riding Limited*	London–Leeds	185.7	2 43	68.4	0	SL

*D Diesel
 S Steam
 P Petrol
 E Electric
 L Loco-hauled

Ahead of its times is this sleek, streamlined, light-weight diesel-powered high-speed express *City of Salina*, seen here on show to an admiring American public in 1935.

Many people who seldom travel very far by train have,
even so, made a life's hobby of studying them, obtaining
much vicarious enjoyment from their acquired knowledge
of journeys by train and railway operations. There is a vast
range of semi-technical literature for the train 'buff'. One
sample is included here, both for its characteristic
catalogue of data and for the way the fascination with detail
tends to overshadow the extraordinary fact that the
journey, as described, took place with a duke at the controls
and a king among the passengers. From Gérard Vuillet
again: 'The most outstanding feat performed by two types
of engines (one French, one German,) was undoubtedly
the run made on the night of 23-24 February 1927, when
the up *Sud-Express*, conveying King Alphonse XIII, left
San Sebastian 1hr 58min late and got into Madrid only
1min late. The delay was due to a hurricane in the French
Landes south of Bordeaux, damaging the track. Thanks to
the courtesy of the late Duke of Zaragoza, who drove the
train himself throughout, I am able to give details of this
extraordinary journey.

'The weight of the train was 248 tons and the engines
used were 4–8–0 No. 4035 to Miranda and 4–8–2 No. 4602
thereafter ... The speed limits varying between 43.5 and
56mph were strictly observed and practically all the time
gained was due to outstanding uphill work ... No. 4602
climbed the 1,555ft from Miranda to km 390.9 in 1hr, up
ruling gradients of 1/87–1/125–1/100. The climb from
Avila to km 98 was extremely fine, the steepest part of the
ascent, between km 116 and km 101, 9.3 miles averaging
1/63 compensated with short stretches at 1/47, being
climbed at 43.5mph. An amusing point was that nobody
could imagine that the train would regain all the lost time,
and when King Alphonse XIII stepped down from his
special car the station was deserted.'

For the traveller, the railway 'buff' or merely for the man
in the street, a journey by rail has for years spelled
romance, drama, excitement. Other forms of travel make
their own strong appeal but, in a sense, more remotely:
until the motor vehicle came to dominate the scenery, the
train, whether the express roaring through its local station

or the suburban train making its halting way across the countryside, came closest to the average man's everyday experience. This awareness, and the proud majesty of some of the great steam locomotives, would set his imagination wandering; and from the stirred imaginations of novelists, poets, dramatists, artists and composers have come many great works, featuring trains in one form or other, to provide entertainment or enlightenment for all.

If one art form predominates, particularly in the 1920s and 1930s, this must be the film. Best known, perhaps, were *Rome Express*, starring Conrad Veidt in a well-told tale of theft and murder; *Shanghai Express*, in which Marlene Dietrich was saved in the nick of time by Clive Brook; and two years later, in 1934, *Orient Express* based on Graham Greene's novel *Stamboul Train*. In this period there were also the *Phantom Express, Exile Express, Berlin Express*, as well as a number of Alfred Hitchcock films in which trains were featured: *The Thirty-Nine Steps, The Secret Agent* and *The Lady Vanishes*.

Hollywood did not, however, have it all its own way.

The British produced *The Flying Scotsman* and *The Last Journey*, while the French may be said to have capped them all with Jean Renoir's *La Bête Humaine*. The latter featured Jean Gabin as a homicidal train driver who murdered his mistress, errant wife of an assistant station master; he then proceeded to bash his fireman into kingdom come before himself leaping suicidally from the train.

Most memories of journeys by train are, we hope, happier than that. The train may not be what it was but it is still with us and, in many ways, evolves and improves as an agreeable means of communication all the time. Only the fabulous, steam-hauled *grands express*, with all their promise of mystery and romance, no longer exist. One cannot imagine Jean Gabin in the driving seat of a modern diesel multi-unit high-speed train. A few years ago he might have been an airline pilot but today, most likely, he would be the driver of our newest form of 'train', the articulated lorry.

A great moment, calling for wine, champagne and cordial handshakes, as the two sections of a new trans-America railway track meet half way across the country.

5 AIR TRAVEL: THE FIRST OF THE MANY

In early 1919 a few former pilots of the Royal Air Force, recovering some old planes from the scrap heap, 'set up in business to give their air-hungry fellow citizens a taste of flying, at a guinea a time'. One of the largest enterprises was at Blackpool, where that summer a five-man team, making between them more than two hundred trips a day, failed to clear the waiting queues. 'When the machines first started people were rather chary about trusting themselves into these strange-looking vehicles, having read so much about the heroism of aviators and the perils of aviation in the Press; but as the machines continued to operate day after day without an accident, and not only made the usual circular trips of a few minutes' duration round Blackpool, but actually flew regularly on a daily service between Blackpool and Manchester, the people began to realise that flying was nothing like as dangerous as they thought it was.' Out of joy-riding grew an appetite for travel by air.

The star turn of any story of the early days of commercial airlines has to be the London–Paris route. At the end of the First World War, these cities were the world's leading diplomatic and commercial capitals. More significantly, however, a stretch of water separated them; and this obstacle, even where it comprised a mere twenty miles across the Straits of Dover, represented a major challenge to the airline operator. Flying people over the sea was to be considered for many years a special peril. At first, it was a question of reaching out to the Continent from Britain; later, of crossing the Mediterranean to Africa; and well into the 1930s, of carrying passengers in buoyant flying boats a step at a time, from one waterside overnight stop to the next, along routes serving the distant possessions of the European colonial powers. By then, even the Pacific was being crossed by a similar island-hopping process but the greatest challenge of all, the crossing of the wide, turbulent North Atlantic, was not met finally until the very eve of the Second World War.

There were psychological reasons as well as those of prestige and economy for the early development of the London–Paris route. Here, in the peacemaking aftermath of war, was the world's greatest concentration of VIP traffic. In economic terms, given comparable fares, the traveller in a hurry could save valuable time by flying from London to Paris by aeroplane in a few short hours. Surface transportation, on the other hand, involved travelling by ship with connecting trains on either side of the Channel, which was much slower. And psychologically, air travel offered escape from the tedium and discomfort, including greater risk of seasickness, to which passengers were exposed on that long-winded and over-boisterous train-ship-train marathon.

One could not say, however, that air travel, even on this VIP-infested route, was exactly luxurious. The first airliners, adapted from wartime bombers, and flown with some abandon by demobilized military aviators, were little more than boxes with windows inserted; and some services started business with open cockpits for pilot and passenger alike. The boxes gave shelter from the elements but at first lacked heating, and there was no communication except by

Smart people were happy to travel, and to be seen to travel, by air as
early as the 1920s.

BUSINESS MEN ARE TAKING TO THE AIR

To cross London the business man uses his own car and it is now just as practical for him to travel across Europe in his own Avro 5.

The Avro 5 is equipped with three 100 h.p. Armstrong-Siddeley engines and has a cruising speed of 100 m.p.h. Its carpeted cabin contains chairs for four people. It is electrically lighted, and comfortably ventilated. There is, in fact, everything necessary for convenient and pleasurable travelling. The Avro 5 can land in 330 yards and can be left anywhere in all weathers. To own one is to be utterly independent of all public transport arrangements and to be able to travel anywhere at any time with speed, safety and comfort.

AVRO·5
(3 ENGINED MONOPLANE)

Left and above: The ultimate status symbol being a privately owned plane. Personal service and glamorous accessories diverted attention from the sometimes rough-and-ready ambience aloft, not to mention the risk of airsickness in the slow, low-flying aircraft of that period.

shouting. Ventilation was provided by the simple means, as in the motor car or train, of lowering the window and letting in the air. It needed time for the influence of the great designers of that period, Britons like Handley Page and De Havilland and the Dutchman Fokker, to be felt; and for a fierce competitive spirit to be translated by market-sensitive operators into sophisticated passenger-cosseting amenities.

Meanwhile, the pioneer aircraft carried a mere handful of passengers, arranged usually in pairs of seats, one behind the other, with a central aisle. With no in-flight services, the earliest devices for distracting the passenger were a map of the route and, perhaps, an altimeter dial. Indeed, one of the attractions of flying at the low speeds and altitudes which then prevailed was the chance to enjoy a leisurely bird's-eye view of familiar landmarks. It was all part of the game if the aircraft, forced down into a convenient field by storms, and continuing its flight when the weather improved, came rather closer to some landmarks than strictly the book allowed.

The first airports serving London and Paris were Hounslow and Le Bourget respectively. A limousine service was usually provided from and to the city centres. For those who wished to eat during the 2½-3-hour flight, a box picnic comprising sandwiches, fruit and chocolate could be bought at the port of departure, though passengers wishing to have a drink en route had to bring their own. From 1920 Croydon, less than thirty minutes away by car, became the principal airport for London.

By 1922 the London–Paris route was catering for over ten thousand passengers in a year, of which three-quarters were being carried by three competing British airlines. This was the year when the first-ever airline steward was appointed; and although planes were still unheated, the amenity of a toilet and, more important, of radio communication with and between individual aircraft, was becoming standard. In 1924, Britain's first national airline, Imperial Airways, was formed by the amalgamation of the competing operators, and the English Channel was now being crossed by regular services connecting London, not only with Paris, but with Amsterdam, Basle, Berlin, Brussels, Cologne and Zurich. In a typical week over sixty planes, half of them British, and the remainder mostly French, Dutch and German, were working in and out of Croydon on the routes from London to the Continent.

The experiences of some of the airline travellers on the London–Paris route were hardly inviting. As John Pudney has recorded in his book *The Seven Skies*, George Stevenson-Reece, travelling in 1919 on the first commercial international scheduled flight, enjoyed the outward journey from London. At two thousand feet 'the Crystal Palace showed like a child's toy'. Then there was mist and, in due course, although Le Bourget was clear enough for landing, 'I search in vain for the Eiffel Tower and Sacré Coeur and try to persuade myself that I like "banking" as we curl downwards to arrive just two hours and twenty minutes after leaving Hounslow'. The return home was a different story. 'I have painfully vivid memories of being

Opposite: Among Britain's best-known *de-luxe* Pullman trains, the *Southern Belle*, en route from London to Brighton, was later renamed *Brighton Belle* and, electrified, became one of the world's earliest multiple-unit 'prestige' expresses.

sick without stopping throughout the return journey to London and ... just as we were landing at 2.45 pm at Hounslow, a last-minute zoom added the final touch and made me grab my hat for a purpose for which in modern air-travel paperbags are thoughtfully provided.'

The nine emergency-landing grounds between London and Paris must have been a great consolation. The main navigational aids were railway lines with place names, in large white letters, painted on the station roofs. A pilot on this pioneer route records gales and storms cancelling one of the early services, 'but ignorant of these conditions I left Paris with two passengers in a DH4 ... When the English coast came into sight, I had had quite enough and decided to land at Lympne.' But conditions there were such 'that we swung off for Hounslow. That journey across Kent was one I would not wish on anybody; heavy rain squalls and driving low cloud accompanied the full gale ... At long last the closed sheds of Hounslow loomed through the rain. The wind indicator was in shreds, but the way trees were lying over left no doubt of the wind's direction ... The sight of my passengers as they emerged will never be forgotten. Beaming all over their faces ... they thanked me for what they thought was a wonderful display of stunting!' For this pleasure each passenger had paid £21 for the single trip, including the road transport at both ends. From such arduous beginnings, the reliability of air travel evolved.

On the smoother side of the coin, another passenger at that time, Captain Bruce Ingram, began his journey from London by Underground train to Hounslow and thence by tram. The aircraft contained four arm-chairs for the passengers, their compartment being 'roofed in by a sliding cover, with windows that could be opened or shut as desired'. After Boulogne 'it was decidedly bumpy, and this bumping gives the feeling that one experiences when a lift suddenly descends and seems to leave part of one's anatomy behind'. However, 'in a short twenty-five minutes more (after landing at Le Bourget) I was transacting the urgent business on which I had come, in an office in the middle of Paris ... One cannot hope to describe adequately the interest, the sense of security and the comfort which such a journey gives to the passenger – to say nothing of the time saved, the avoidance of inconveniences caused by the change from train to boat.'

From 1922, to foster public interest, 'all the airline operators indulged in every form of publicity. Press flights were frequent. American publicists and journalists were particularly welcome.' So, when the famous American lecturer Lowell Thomas wanted a flight to Germany, red-carpet treatment was laid on; and when it was realized 'that the American was to be the sole passenger aboard and was thus unlikely to be impressed by the popularity of the new

The SOUTHERN BELLE

"One hour of luxurious travel."

between

LONDON & BRIGHTON

from
VICTORIA

· Weekdays ·
at 11.0 a.m.
& 3.10 p.m.
· Sundays ·
at 11.0 a.m
& 6.30 p.m.

from
BRIGHTON

· Weekdays ·
at 1.20 p.m.
& 5.45 p.m.
· Sundays ·
at 5.0 p.m.
& 9.30 p.m.

London Brighton & South Coast Railway
London Bridge Terminus,
September 1911.

WILLIAM FORBES
General Manager

Opposite above: Before the days of restaurant cars there was a mad scramble for food when trains stopped for refreshments. A scene at a French railway station buffet in 1864.

Opposite below: In the heyday of the railway the station was often both a city's status symbol and a cathedral of national economic advancement, as this view of Washington's Union Terminus suggests.

Right: Happy landings and easy-going formalities in the pre-Jumbo Jet age: a 1921 view of the customs hall at Croydon Airport following the arrival of an airliner from Paris.

service, orders went out at once for members of the airline staff to be dressed as passengers to join the airliner at Croydon and accompany the great man on his journey ... The bad moment came with their arrival when the members of the airline staff in Germany were suddenly confronted by a troop of their own English colleagues doing their best to act the parts of passengers and diligently cutting them dead.'

An enthusiastic airline publicity booklet of that year was not too wide of the mark with its statement: 'Once you have flown to Paris, you will never go by boat again.' The advantages were spelt out: 'It stands to reason that a means by which you gain a useful morning in London, and arrive unjaded in Paris for afternoon tea, in time, maybe, to pay an important business call, or with leisure to do a little sightseeing before dinner, is worth some consideration.' A description of a 'typical' trip follows. 'On reaching the aerodrome ... we notice that the two propellors of one of the several machines standing about are steadily turning ... also we notice that on no face is there an anxiety or doubt ... Passports examined, we approach the machine ... and we step up the neat little steel ladder and into the cabin, an attendant indicating the place. There is a comfortable wicker chair by an ample window ... We observe a door which communicates with the pilot's "office"; and at the opposite end ... is another door with the inscription "Lavatory".'

In the following years, according to Mr G H Steer, a British airline steward, Imperial Airways' passenger lists might include the Prince of Wales, King Alphonso, Winston Churchill, Field Marshal Smuts, Mr Gulbenkian, Shaliyapin and numerous stage and film personalities. The Prince of Wales, always an innovator, often used the aeroplane to go about his business *and* his pleasure: one day in February 1932 he flew from Berkshire to Leicestershire to hunt with the Quorn, and the following day, in their Colonel-in-Chief's attire, he made a cross-country flight to inspect a battalion of the Royal Scots Fusiliers.

Imperial Airways, well forward in the public relations game, soon adopted the practice of publishing lists of its 'most interesting and distinguished passengers'. As Kenneth Hudson in his book *Air Travel, A Social History* reports, Imperial Airways, among numerous foreign 'royals', was laying claim to King Feisal of Iraq and, nearer home, a mere step or two down the social ladder, to Prince Walkonsky, Lord Londonderry, Lord Lymington, Baron Rothschild, Count Spezia, Lady Carlisle, Baroness Doiney, film producer René Clair, boxer Primo Carnera and racing driver Kaye Don.

In 1928 Imperial Airways declared itself proud of 'the enterprise of a party of American businessmen ... who visited Paris, Cologne, Hanover, Berlin, Prague, Vienna, Budapest, Basle and London all in fourteen days, a trip

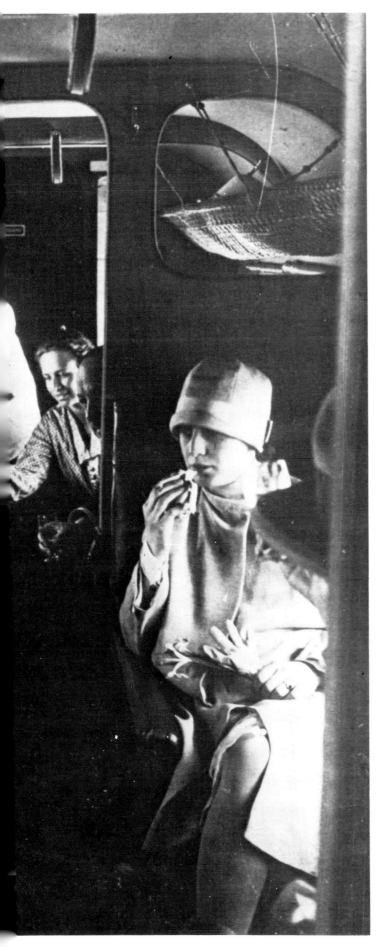

A cinema show in flight was all very well and, indeed, in the 1920s, no mean achievement, but to keep warm the sensible man remained snugly inside his overcoat. By the 1930s luxury aloft, modelled on Pullman train standards, was being taken for granted: (left) shows dinner being served on board a Berlin to Vienna airliner.

impossible by any other form of transport'. In the same year Mr S Donoghue, the famous jockey, 'rode in the 2 o'clock race at Windsor and in a race at 4.30 at Ostend on the same day', the trip beginning with a row 'across the river to a meadow where a fast aeroplane awaited him'. And there was the case involving a London surgeon 'who, having received an urgent summons, flew from Croydon to Le Touquet, and performed a successful operation two hours after leaving Croydon'.

In the early 1930s Imperial Airways made a feature of special Sunday day-trips from Croydon to Le Touquet with lunch and tea in France and dinner on the way home. Propaganda flights over Paris in the first four-engined airliners also proved good for British prestige. For a while, by charging more for the most conveniently timed flights, sheep and goats flew separately. 'The airlines were faced with the always-difficult problem of trying to appeal to an élite and to everybody, at the same time. They had to say, on the one hand, "Everybody flies nowadays", and, on the other, "All the best people fly".' The leading airports were also in competition. From the mid-1920s Le Bourget accommodated passengers on the first floor, with fine views of the airfield, waiting-rooms, bookstall, bank, post office and telephone booths. From 1928, Croydon offered a rather grandly civilized, domed booking-hall and a paved forecourt.

While the British pioneered the airborne lavatory, the Continentals were attending to more inspiring matters. To

Above: Britain's Imperial
Airways proudly presents to VIP
previewers its *Hannibal*, the
world's largest and most
luxurious airliner and (right) a
scene at Croydon, 1931, before an
inaugural flight over London.

Competition was always swift on the prestigious London to Paris run,
with Britain's Imperial Airways more often than not the pace-setter.

xxxvi   PUNCH ALMANACK FOR 1935.   November 5, 1934

TO PARIS WHILE YOU READ YOUR PAPER **AND HOME AGAIN**
THE SAME DAY!

NEARLY 1,700 PERSONS FLY BETWEEN LONDON & PARIS EVERY WEEK

The luxury of Imperial Airways' air liners is proverbial. Pullman-like comfort, meals, attentive stewards, lavatories and luggage space. For you, the chops of the Channel look like ripples and you arrive in Paris fresh and unfatigued, having spent no more time in the air than it takes to run your car from London to lunch with your cousins in the country. Air travel is not expensive and it is very delightful —try it !

LONDON TO PARIS
FROM . £4.15.0
RETURN . £7.12.0

IMPERIAL AIRWAYS
THE GREATEST AIR SERVICE IN THE WORLD

Bookings and information about Imperial Airways travel from the principal travel agents or from Airways Terminus, Victoria Station, S.W.1, or Imperial Airways Ltd., Airways House, Charles Street, Lower Regent Street, S.W.1.   Telephone: VICtoria 2211 (Day & Night).   Telegrams: 'Impairlim, London.'

the Germans, followed closely by the French, goes the credit for introducing hot in-flight meals. As a French menu card for 1927 shows, elaborate meals, accompanied by champagne, red and white wine, whisky, mineral waters and coffee, were a major attraction:

Hors d'œuvre
Langouste Parisienne
Poulet Sauté Chasseur
Jambon d' York à la Gelée
Salade Niçoise
Glace Plombière
Fromages
Corbeille de Fruits

The Imperial Airways advertisement of its London–Paris route at that time offered a touch of romance as well as reassurance, but carefully said nothing about gastronomy. 'Punctuality is part of efficiency, and British efficiency in the air is the standard by which aerial standards are set. You forget the urge (of getting to Paris or London quickly) in the sheer pleasure of an experience that makes 150

minutes the shortest two hours and a half you have ever spent. Really, it is like nothing so much as sitting in the armchair of a Pullman car which suddenly takes to itself wings. You have the same comfort, the same safety and the same convenience even down to the same light refreshments on the way. Ventilation can be adjusted to each individual passenger's liking. If it is cold, the air is warmed. Outside you can hear the hum of the three giant engines . . . unsurpassed by the products of any other makers that the world's air industry has produced.'

However, the French example was bound to be followed one way or another. At first, according to Mr Steer, lunch comprised 'hot soup in Thermos jars . . . There were snacks afterwards – sandwiches, biscuits and cheese, coffee, tea and Bovril; just enough to keep the passengers interested; oh yes – then there was a small bar containing whisky, gin, beer and mineral waters . . .' A little later 'something first-class' was enjoyed and after 'soup or hors-d'œuvre, there was salmon mayonnaise, or something like that, then we gave the passengers a choice of something hot or cold in winter; then there was sweet, cheese, fresh fruit and coffee – a seven-course in all. Sweets were jellies, stewed fruit and

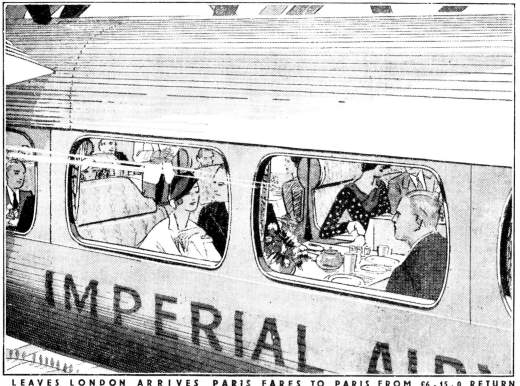

To Paris— while you lunch . . .

By the time you have finished the excellent lunch served in the mid-day *Silver Wing*, soon after leaving Croydon you will be at the outskirts of Paris! Fresh and unfatigued after swift and luxurious travel; with many hours in hand for business or pleasure. Or you can leave London early in the morning, have breakfast on the aeroplane and arrive in Paris with the whole day before you, and then fly back the same evening, dining on the way. Everyone should enjoy the tremendous advantages of travel by these great Imperial Airways liners with their well-served meals, buffets, attentive stewards, and lavatory accommodation. You will appreciate the comfort and speed of the air. Do not just *think* about air travel. *Try* it. Remember Imperial Airways is the fastest service between London and Paris

And send your freight & mail by air too

LEAVES LONDON	ARRIVES PARIS	FARES TO PARIS FROM £6.15.0 RETURN
Airway Terminus (Opposite Continental Departure platform), Victoria Station	Hotel Bohy-Lafayette, Square Montholon—in the heart of Paris.	Book at any Travel Agency or from Imperial Airways, Ltd., Airway Terminus, Victoria Station (facing entrance to Continental Departure platform), S W 1, or Airways House, Charles Street, Lower Regent Street, W.1. Telephone: Victoria 2211 (Night and Day). Telegrams: 'Impairlim London'
daily 7.45 am, 11.45 am and 5.15 pm	**at 11.30 am, 3.30 pm and 9 pm**	

IMPERIAL AIRWAYS

Paris: Airways House, 38 Avenue de l'Opéra.   *Alexandria*: Marine Air Port, Ras-el-Tin, P O Box 1705.   *Karachi*: Karachi Air Port.   *Cape Town*: Wingfield Aerodrome.   *New York*: The Plaza, Fifth Avenue and 59th Street.

THE BRITISH AIR LINE

Stuarts

This picture shows how resemblance to train travel, with emphasis on first-class service by attentive stewards, was considered an asset in advertisements of the 1930s.

cream, small apple tarts with custard or cream . . . The teas were very fine, especially coming out of Paris, when we had on board a first-class variety of sandwiches and French pastries.' This was the kind of improving treatment offered by Imperial Airways' *Silver Wing Service*, setting 'the standard of luxury in travel by air'; and it flew both ways every day of the year (except Christmas) leaving the centre of each city at 11.10 to reach the centre of the other at 15.15.

Ethel Mannin, a regular Imperial Airways supporter, recalls that the airline 'thoughtfully provides each passenger with an aluminium cuspidor – cardboard cartons on German planes and paper bags on the French machines'. But 'no privacy was possible in the event of air sickness' and this was even more so in 'the new super-Hannibal machines because then you had a passenger facing you'. Clearly, this lady's sense of the absurd overcame her apprehensions. On another occasion, flying to France, 'the sun was shining when we left Croydon but before we reached the coast we ran into rain, and flew so low that we terrified chickens, horses, cattle, who fled in all directions'. At Brussels 'I had a coffee and cigarette with

the pilot at the aerodrome café; he asked me if I was on this stage, and I asked *him* if we should make the journey'.

O P Marland recalls: 'In June 1935 I went across from London to Paris in a Handley Page machine called a Hannibal. It had four motors spread among the sticks and strings which held the two wings of the bi-plane together. The fuselage was slung underneath and there were wonderful views from the windows, as there were no wings to get in the way. It was spacious and comfortable, but very slow – about 90 mph. I remember seeing a Douglas DC3 of Swissair or maybe KLM alongside and climbing, just after take off from Croydon. When it levelled off it went forward like a rocket and made us look as if we were hovering.'

In February of 1937 and 1938 Marland, on skiing holidays, 'flew to Zurich in Swissair DC3 aircraft both times. The DC3 had two Wright Cyclone motors and was very fast for those days (180/190 mph). It took 21 people, 14 on one side, double-banked and 7 on the other. It was the first commercial aircraft ever to have a retractable undercarriage.'

And Graham Greene describes how 'the Royal Dutch plane swung off the ground, treading air ... Fred Hall stuck the cotton-wool in his ears .... He knew the airports of Europe as well as he had once known the stations on the Brighton line – shabby Le Bourget; the great scarlet

Speed has always been a good
selling-point and, accordingly, a
main determinant of aircraft
design. In the 1930s the
beginnings of modern aircraft
shapes appeared: in (above) the
Hispano-Suiza *Emeraude*, 'most
talked-of aeroplane of 1934',
about to leave Paris for Moscow;
and (right) a Savoia-Marchetti,
making history with its capability
of Paris to Rome and back in one
day.

rectangle of the Tempelhof as one came in from London in the dark, the headlamp lighting up the asphalt way; the white sand blowing up round the shed at Tallin; Riga, where the Berlin to Leningrad plane came down and bright pink mineral waters were sold in a tin-roofed shed; the huge aerodrome at Moscow with machines parked half a dozen deep ... The engines were shut off, and the sudden silence pressed on the ears through the wads of cotton-wool. They sank through deep cloud towards a dark-green sea ... The ten minutes' wait at Copenhagen seemed like an hour ... and then at Malmö there was more delay.'

Europe, if not the world, was now the air traveller's oyster.

Although the flying boat, soon to become the main means of long-distance air travel, was about to come into its stride in the mid-1920s, with Britain and Germany setting the pace, several authorities held that the future of intercontinental travel lay primarily with the airship. According to Nevil Shute, 'it was generally agreed in 1924 that the aeroplane would never be a very suitable vehicle for carrying passengers across the oceans, and that airships would operate all the long-distance routes of the future'. At this time, certainly, when the airship alone had enough endurance for non-stop ocean-wide flights without refuelling, only this type of conveyance could hold sway over the coveted North Atlantic route. Here the acknowledged leaders, with the famous Zeppelins, were the Germans, their *Graf Zeppelin* making its first flight in 1928.

These vast, lighter-than-air dirigibles offered spacious passenger accommodation and amenities rather like those

For several years, the airship was the only conveyance capable of direct non-stop ocean-wide flights; and in this sphere the Germans became the acknowledged leaders. Their *Graf Zeppelin*, introduced in 1928 for the North Atlantic service, is seen here (below) moored at Lakehurt, New Jersey; (right) in flight over Buckingham Palace, London.

The *Graf Zeppelin* passes the Pyramids on a Near East cruise.

provided by ocean liners, with the advantage of smoother motion and higher speeds. Indeed, the most valued characteristic of the airship was probably its serene detachme⸬ f⸬ ⸬ the heaving elements above which it flew. The sweet life aloft was, however, hampered somewhat by stringent safety restrictions; and it was not until 1936, when the *Hindenburg* came on the scene, that passengers were permitted to smoke in flight. Even then, the only person allowed the custody of matches was the steward in charge of the sealed-off, double-doored smoking compartment. As a special concession to pipe and cigar smokers, this steward could usually be prevailed upon to light a match on condition that he, personally, held it 'from ignition to charred cinder'. A single electric lighter was provided for cigarette smokers.

Between smokes, passengers in small groups were invariably given a thorough guided tour of the ship. Kenneth Hudson writes that 'none failed to be impressed by the vast dimensions of the gas cells, the quantities of stores, fuel and water carried on each side of the narrow catwalk, and the reassuring presence of the spare engine and reserve propellers, all lending a sense of permanence and purpose'.

The *Hindenburg*'s dining-room, seating thirty-four passengers, had 'all the luxury and refinement of a small restaurant ... The chairs were upholstered, there were attractive paintings on the walls and the tables were laid with white linen knapkins and tablecloths, fresh-cut flowers, fine silver and the special china service created for the *Hindenburg*.'

Across the way was the lounge, bearing 'a huge Mercator

Pictures captioned 'Hotel Life in the Air' taken aboard the German Zeppelin *Hindenburg*, 'the largest airship ever built', during its maiden flight from Europe to South America in 1936.

FOLLOWING THE AIRSHIP'S FLIGHT ON A DECORATIVE WALL-MAP: PASSENGERS
ON BOARD THE "HINDENBURG" POINTING TO THEIR DESTINATION IN BRAZIL.

LOOKING DOWN ON THE OCEAN FROM AN OBSERVATION WINDOW: A GROUP INCLUDING
DR. HUGO ECKENER (THIRD FROM LEFT), THE AIRSHIP'S FAMOUS COMMANDER.

ALL THE AMENITIES OF HOTEL LIFE IN CLOUDLAND: A TYPICAL COMPANY
IN THE DINING-SALOON OF THE "HINDENBURG" DURING LUNCHEON.

THE RULING PASSION STRONG IN FLIGHT: TWO PASSENGERS IN THE "HINDENBURG"
ABSORBED IN A GAME OF CHESS, WHILE ANOTHER WATCHES THE SEA.

THE new Zeppelin "Hindenburg," the largest airship ever built, recently completed
her maiden flight across the South Atlantic to Brazil and back, and though
on the return journey, when over the Mediterranean, two engines proved defective,
she reached Friedrichshafen, on April 10, only an hour behind her scheduled time.
Because of this engine trouble, it may be recalled, she wirelessed for permission to
fly over France instead of across the Alps, and this was granted by the French
Premier, M. Sarraut. The "Hindenburg" carried 36 passengers (including 7 women), a

Britain's airship efforts culminated in the 1930s in the ill-fated R.101, seen here (left) at its mooring mast at Cardington, England. The view of this vessel's somewhat spartan lounge (above) conveys, correctly if unwittingly, an air of fragility and impermanence.

projection of the world, depicting the ships and sea voyages of Columbus, Vasco da Gama, Magellan and Cook, the North Atlantic route of the German express liners *Bremen* and *Europa*, the Atlantic crossing of the LZ126 *Los Angeles*, the world flight of the *Graf Zeppelin* and so on. There was even a Bluthner baby grand piano, its weight kept down to 397lbs through the use of aluminium, and finished in yellow pigskin.'

There were also a writing- and reading-room and a library, while outboard of the public rooms were two fifty-foot promenades which, with the connecting cross passage, 'afforded a walking distance of nearly two hundred feet for transatlantic passengers used to the daily constitutional around a steamer deck'. Through the windows lighting the promenades 'the passengers stood or sat for hours on low cushioned seats, enthralled by the sight of foaming waves, tossing ships . . . going by only a few hundred feet below'. The amenities of the cabins were, of coarse, in keeping, including 'three push buttons, the lower one identified by a wine glass. When you pushed it a drink was produced'.

But a mere dozen years or so proved to be the heyday of the airship, with its vulnerability to fire and, when berthing, high winds. In the 1930s calamitous accidents affected British as well as German airships with substantial loss of life but, although there was still no heavier-than-air machine capable of a regular, non-stop transatlantic crossing, the flying boat was now so well established on other routes, and the technological prospect for land planes so promising, that few tears were shed for the departing species.

The first flying boat to make a substantial contribution to long-distance travel was Britain's Short Singapore, introduced in 1926. This was the aircraft used by Sir Alan Cobham in a round-Africa flight to prove how the British

Empire could well be linked by air services. At this time a Briton could get himself to the Persian Gulf by a regular service, involving air travel part of the way: having reached Marseilles by train he would take a ship to Egypt, thence a train to Cairo and on by air, via Gaza and Rutbah Wells, to Baghdad. Three years later, despite a risk of forced landings in the desert with the possibility of being held hostage by armed tribesmen, this route was extended to India, with the following stages: London–Basle by air, thence due to over-flying restrictions by train to Genoa, and on by air via Alexandria, Cairo and Baghdad to Karachi. This was a great step forward in comfort and convenience, and good value at £130 for the seven-day journey.

In 1930 it fell to a German to be the first to fly the Atlantic westward by flying boat but by now the British were a long way ahead with the development of routes to be served by this type of aircraft. In early 1931 Imperial Airways opened the first commercial route from London to central Africa, using a land plane to Athens, a flying boat from Athens to Alexandria and a land plane across Egypt and the Sudan. By the end of that year experimental flights were being made right through to Cape Town.

Within a few years this trans-Africa service was being operated largely by four-engined flying boats with surprisingly spacious accommodation. This, and the attentive service, 'are still recalled with great affection by the people who travelled in them ... The (Short) Empire flying boat offered exceptional amenities ... There was, for instance, a smoking cabin.' The other cabins included one amidships, adjoining the kitchen and toilets; another, further astern, a large 'promenade cabin seating eight or resting four. On the port side is a rail for elbow-resting by the windows and a surprising amount of space for promenading ... and behind it a further cabin with six seats for daylight flying or sleeping accommodation for four ... Every bunk has a little window above it with a cover flap and by each row of seats are universally mounted hot and cold air intakes and a light incorporating a switch and a bell-push.'

In the later Frobishers, a land plane species, there were three passenger compartments 'carpeted richly and deeply ... with sofa-like double seats on either side of the through walk down the middle'. Available free to passengers were, among other pleasures, 'cocoa, coffee, chocolate, Bovril, sandwiches, cocktail snacks, biscuits, fresh fruit ... aspirin, smelling salts, eau de Cologne, Enos Fruit Salts ... air sickness tablets, soap and towels. There was also, of course, a full, grand-hotel-style catering service at the main meal-times.'

Enthusiastic nannies near Southampton interest the future generation in a British flying boat of the 1930s, mainstay of long-distance aerial communications in those last hours of the imperial heyday.

Even so, in the mid-1930s there were many difficulties to be met. On the branch east–west service between the Sudan and Nigeria 'as there were then no radio direction facilities, it became necessary for all flying to be done during the daylight hours ... After leaving Khartoum, and calling at El Geninena and El Obeid, the Service had to make a night stop at El Fasher, and then proceed the following day to Kano, calling at Fort Lamy and Maiduguri en route.'

When flying from west to east, with only two days for the trip, the machines had to be ready 'with all passengers, mails and air freight aboard at both Kano and El Fasher by 5.30 a.m. on the day of their departure ...' Then there was the justifiable fear of the spread of Yellow Fever from Nigeria. 'In order to meet the requirements of the Health Authorities of the Sudan, it was necessary at each stop (in Nigeria) for the plane itself, each member of the crew and each individual passenger to be well sprayed by a Health Department Official, before anybody was allowed even to leave the plane ... Eventually, a very Senior Official from Nigeria, who had been over for talks in the Sudan, on returning to the Colony, received the full blast of spray in the face on his arrival at Maiduguri, and thereafter, the severity of the procedure was very much modified.'

Progress had been swift also along the other main imperial route, the more so since its operators, the Dutch, were in strong competition with the British, with Batavia and Singapore respectively as the interim destinations. As early as 1926 Lady Maud Hoare, wife of the British cabinet minister, had set a standard for VIP travel by accompanying her husband on a flight from London to India despite 'personal problems for a pioneer woman passenger travelling such a distance with so many stops at which she had to make official appearances as the Air Minister's wife. No-one had ever thought of lightweight aviation luggage for instance.' Having found a substitute for the heavy leather of which most baggage was made in those days, and flimsy containers for the various glass bottles and china pots containing cosmetics, Lady Hoare was able to reduce her wardrobe to 'a stockinette coat and skirt, with a *crêpe-de-chine* jumper ... a woollen jumper and tweed skirt as a change ... and according to temperature, woollen cardigan, leather coat and fur coat. The felt hat matched the coat and skirt and gum boots were occasionally most useful on wet aerodromes. A black lace evening dress for formal dinner parties ... and a demi-toilette completed the visible list; but my most cherished possession was a Shetland dressing-gown.' By modern standards, a somewhat heavy-weight light weight!

On the whole, the Dutch were ahead of the British in the early stages of this game, opening the first regular passenger service from Amsterdam to Batavia in 1930 with four-seater aircraft. The journey, occupying twelve days, involved numerous stops, including Budapest, Athens, Cairo, Baghdad, Bushire, Jask, Karachi, Jodhpur, Allahabad, Calcutta, Akyab, Rangoon, Bangkok, Medan and Palembang. Fuel, board and lodging were provided at hotels en route and, to make the bureaucrats happy, passengers were obliged to have the correct visas for each country where the planes landed. By 1935 the Dutch airline KLM could claim an annual load of 1,500 passengers on this prestigious route.

Widely publicized flying contests, and the annual race by sea planes for the Schneider Trophy and the England–Australia race of 1934, were important spurs. The latter, with entrants from Australia, Britain, Denmark, Eire, Holland, New Zealand and the United States, twenty-one planes in all, slashed the accepted flying time from Europe to the Far East. The winner, a British aircraft, left Mildenhall at 0634 on 20 October, and reached Melbourne at 0535 on 23 October. The machine, a Comet DH 88 was a twin-engined monoplane built mainly of wood, with a cockpit for two with dual controls, but only one set of instruments.

This race was 'a unique event in aviation history ... paving the way for long-distance commercial aviation and making a powerful impact on strategic concepts. It ... spurred development of a revolutionary British aircraft, the Comet DH 88. It brought to world notice the great aircraft companies Douglas and Boeing ... It established the reputation of KLM Royal Dutch Airlines.'

In 1933 Imperial Airways opened its route from London to Singapore. Having completed ten million miles of flying and, with the accident insurance rate for air travel reduced from 12s to 1s per £1,000, it could claim to be as safe as surface travel. Two years later reliable connections were provided from Singapore through Darwin to Brisbane and from Penang through Saigon to Hong Kong, the time in transit from London to the latter colony being only ten days.

The cosy life aloft, both British-style and Dutch, suffered numerous interruptions. The route to Brisbane involved thirty-five landings. According to passengers' reports of flights in the mid-1930s, in North Australia 'the temperature rose 16° in the four minutes we were on the ground'. With the temperature at 96°, sausage rolls were served for lunch and, at another stop, 'hot omelettes and macaroni, hot peas and salmon, tinned fruit and mineral waters'. Then, 'at the end of each day there were cars waiting to take us to good comfortable hotels – the hotels at Medan, Jodhpur and Athens were even surprising in their comfort ... If any objection is to be made it is that we were offered in fact too much to eat ... It was not merely a question of the early snacks, breakfasts, luncheons and afternoon teas, but on board we were continually offered tea, coffee or beef-tea with sandwiches and biscuits.' In the aircraft, the chairs 'can be transformed into veritable couches; there is so much leg room that at the foot-end two suit-cases can be placed on end, one behind the other, without interfering with the chair in front. High up in the air, it is cool and well-ventilated and everyone sleeps or reads or nibbles at something ... One of the pleasant things ... was the absence of noise in the cabin ... The engine hum is certainly heard, but it is not annoying and I could easily converse with my fellow passengers and there was no need to plug up my ears with cotton wool.'

Train travel has long provided a venue of jokes and saucy humour, as witness this 1926 drawing from *La Vie Parisienne* captioned, 'I hope you don't mind me smoking.'

Air travel in Europe: two scenes at Paris Le Bourget Aerodrome in
1934. (Above), passengers for London embark in an Imperial Airways
Handley Page air liner; (below), an Air France Farman disembarking
passengers from Amsterdam.

But, down to earth: in a rest-house on Lombok Island 'there were about three bedrooms, each containing a huge Dutch bed into which two or even three people had to be piled when there was a good load of passengers. The usual "Dutch wife" was of course placed down the centre of the bed and at least served to keep the occupants apart. The lavatory amenities consisted of one cubicle with two holes in the ground and a row of bottles of water.'

Generally, however, all this was often preferred to rail travel. After one of these flights, on a journey by train from London to Liverpool, 'the first thing that strikes me is the noise of this train ... The next thing is the unsteadiness – my cup of tea has spilt itself ... Then I can't see anything from here; the windows are steamed over, but when I wipe one I find the smoke from the engine obliterating the view ... It certainly isn't as comfortable – I can put my feet up on a newspaper on the opposite seat, but I still have an almost upright back to the seat; the carriage is badly ventilated and no one has ever claimed for train travel that it is clean! And now, as a climax, I find that ... this train is half-an-hour late at Lime Street.'

In the late 1930s, the Short Empire flying boats became Imperial Airways' best-known asset. In 1936, forty-four of these aircraft were ordered by the British airline, and within two years, they were being employed on seven passenger flights a week to Egypt, four to India, three to East Africa and two each to South Africa, Malaya, Hong Kong and Australia.

The pattern of Imperial Airways' regular intercontinental routes by 1939 can be seen in the table (right).

Then, in August 1939, using the Empire flying boat, Imperial Airways offered a mail service from Britain to the United States, with a non-stop flying time of fifteen hours between Shannon and Botwood, the prelude to a regular passenger service. Great progress but, alas, the Second World War was only days away. . . .

During these years the Americans had been far from idle in the development of long-distance routes, though strangely, until the late 1920s, they lagged behind the leading European nations in the development of civil aviation nearer home. According to Ernest Gann, 'The entire circumstance of American air transport was disgraceful ... We were so far behind the rest of the world ... Imperial Airways had long been flying passengers in cocktail and full dinner-service luxury ... Air France ... offered fairly reliable services across the Sahara ... Royal Dutch Airlines flew half way round the world ... Lufthansa was everywhere ... and even the confused Italians operated a regular service across the South Atlantic ... We were still held in such distrust that many large firms forbade their executives to fly.'

On the face of it, America's hesitant start may seem surprising in view of the relatively large size of the United States and the smaller density there of roads and railways. But distance provided the problem as well as the challenge until aircraft could fly at night and the range of aircraft be increased to offer non-stop flights able to compete on a

Britain's Imperial Airways: Summary of Intercontinental Routes on Eve of the Second World War

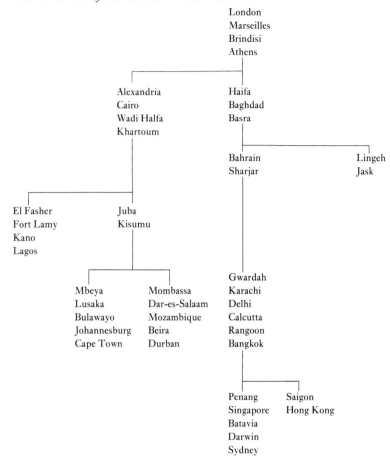

lengthy journey with the express train. And the Americans had, among other obstacles, the Rockies which, in the early stages of the aeroplane's evolution, offered hazards comparable in severity with those of the open sea.

Although the first non-stop cross-country flight had been made in 1923, the best that could be managed coast-to-coast at the end of the 1920s, by Transcontinental Air Transport, the predecessor of TWA, was a forty-eight hour transit involving an overnight journey by train from New York to Columbus, Ohio; then a daytime flight by aircraft to Waynoka, Oklahoma; another night in a train; and a final hop from Clovis, New Mexico, to Los Angeles. At the start of the 1930s the transit time was reduced to thirty-six hours comprising two-day flights by air separated by one overnight stop. In 1932 the final barrier, that of night flying, being overcome by the rather costly means of a lit emergency-landing ground every twenty miles, the transit time fell to a mere twenty-four hours.

However, the real breakthrough came in 1935 when the insurance companies decided that air travel was now safe enough for the valuable bodies of Hollywood film stars to be entrusted to it. By this time, sophistication and glamour as well as performance were becoming the watchword. F Scott Fitzgerald wrote: 'Airports lead you way back in history like oases, like the stops on the great trade routes. The sight of air travellers strolling in ones and twos into midnight airports will draw a small crowd any night up to

In its heyday the flying boat, backbone of long-distance air routes, offered space, reliability and, once aboard, warmth and comfort. The process of disembarkation was often, however, distinctly rugged (above). The giant Dormier flying boat (left) at Southampton, after crossing the Atlantic in 1932, seems a huge weight for its puny engines: but it worked!

Ellen Church, the first of a large, ever-growing, worldwide family of air hostesses, took up her duties aboard a Boeing 80A of America's United Airlines in 1930.

A typical short-haul maid-of-all-work biplane airliner of the early 1930s: the Imperial Airways *Heracles* in graceful and leisurely flight above Manchester Airport in 1932.

two. The young people look at the planes, the older ones look at the passengers with a watchful incredulity. In the big trans-continental planes we (from Hollywood) were the coastal rich, who casually alighted from our cloud in mid-America. High adventure might be among us, disguised as a movie star.'

In 1933 the Boeing 247, regarded by some authorities as the first modern transport plane, had come into service, reducing the coast-to-coast transit time to under twenty-four hours. This twin-engined all-metal monoplane, with a load of ten passengers, was able to cruise at 155 mph at a height of 18,000 feet and had a range of 500 miles. Then, as a spur to competition, the Douglas DC–1 aircraft came on the market with characteristics very similar to those of the Boeing 247 but, marginally, a better performance. And soon, as Marland reminds us, there would be sleeping planes. 'In December 1939 I flew out from New York on an overnight sleeper air service to spend Christmas in San Francisco. It was a DC3, operated by United Airlines. To give everyone a sleeping berth, the numbers were cut down to 14, that is 7 each side.

'At night the whole plane was converted to upper and lower berths, really very comfortable beds – 6′ 6″ long, with sheets and blankets. You undressed, as you did on the Pullman trains, in the berth, hanging your clothes on all sorts of clever devices, built for the purpose. Then you donned your pyjamas and settled down. All stewardesses in those days had to be trained nurses and they also did the making up and stowing of the berths. In the morning you awoke to a very good breakfast ... No crowds, no hustle and bustle. The passenger was a very special person who was transported by car at airports, cosseted at every point, fed and wined in fine fashion. When making a flight, you gave your hotel or home phone number to the airline and they phoned each passenger at least once on the day, to confirm the take-off.'

Meanwhile, the American overseas initiatives had got off to a fair start in 1920 with an air service linking Florida with Havana and, following Charles Lindbergh's historic solo Atlantic crossing, the Americans forged ahead with longer distance services. In the pioneering stages, 'when we established more north and south flights between Miami and bases on the north coast of South America, then flights linking these bases, pushing farther around the bulge of the continent and down the east coast ... the Indians stole our wind-socks for pants, whanged curare-dipped arrows at our low-flying aircraft and grinned at us with filed teeth while we sweated it out on some small field during frequent long layovers waiting for some needed part to arrive ... Food at our ports of call was of such poor quality that we learned to carry a supply of beans, tomatoes and fruit juice to last the round trip ...'

In 1930 Pan Am was offering two different routes to Buenos Aires and a few years later a flying-boat service down the east coast of South America. Pan Am's growth had been rapid: in 1927 it had a single one-hundred-mile route; by 1936, using the Martin 130 China Clipper, it had conquered the Pacific with a service from San Francisco through Honolulu, Midway, Wake Island and Guam to Manila, with a branch to Hong Kong from 1937.

In the other direction, closing the final gap, Pan Am started regular mail services in 1938 from New York to Marseilles via Lisbon and, finally, to Southampton via Newfoundland. The plane on these most prestigious routes was the famous Boeing 314 Yankee Clipper. Thus, to the Americans, as winners by a short head of the North Atlantic race, went the ultimate prize. However, nearly ten years would pass before this early trickle could become a stream which would rapidly broaden into the torrent of today. As for the last pre-war word about the two great contenders of that era, let Cy Caldwell the American aeronautical journalist, writing in 1939, have it: 'As we took off from Croydon the steward handed around wine lists; everybody ignored them and ordered Scotch and soda or bottled ale ...' Soon, 'hardy Britons were eating Consommé Julienne, fricassée of chicken, roast fillet of veal, ham and egg salad, and cheese, Gorgonzola, Cheddar or Cheshire ... In slightly less than an hour and a half everyone had been filled up with something, the dishes and glasses were whisked away, nearly everyone was smoking and we were gliding down ... to Le Bourget. I was sorry to get out; it had been like sitting in a comfortable friendly club. It is the English genius for being human and understanding with air travellers that makes Imperial Airways one of the best liked services in the world. This is not only my impression; several other travellers, mostly Americans, also felt the same way.'

Fifty years after it all began, jostled but not surpassed by the ever-growing worldwide bands of competitors, that old, tough but friendly, neck-and-neck contest continues.

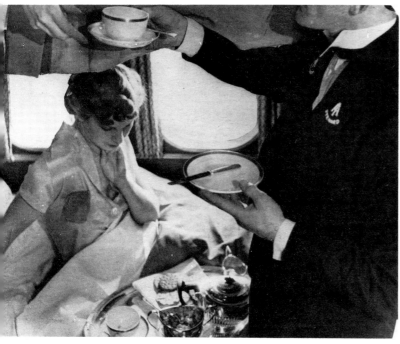

Above: After an overnight flight in comfortable beds, passengers enjoy breakfast on a tray aboard a 1930s flying boat: only the best silver and chinaware was good enough!

Below: Children inspect the cockpit of a Hercules airliner during its call at Malta in 1926 en route from London to Cairo, with mail and passengers for the Gulf and India.

Right: Something to write home about, indeed: a cheerful group of American women students are delighted to find themselves safely in London after their flight from Paris in 1922.

6 ROAD TRAVEL IN THE OLD WORLD

The sweet life, 1920s fashion:
three stylish ladies of leisure
enjoy a sunny, gossipy picnic
during a day at the motor car
races at the Brooklands, England,
track.

1919 was a great year for the motor car. In Europe, where cars were still largely a luxury or a hobby, survivors from the battlefields vied with war profiteers to put their money into a set of wheels: the wave of post-war optimism was generating a spending spree. Women, too, were in the market for the first time, muscle power being no longer needed to set a car in motion. Having watched a friend die from the effects of cranking his car, Henry C Leland, one of America's most versatile carmakers, had invented the electric starter; from 1918, it was part of the available equipment in Ford's famous maid-of-all-work, the T model.

Although during the First World War France had suffered greater devastation than any other country and the best engineering brains had concentrated on developing machines for war, this remained for a while the natural home of the classic car, *la voiture de grand luxe*, with lessons learned from developing aero engines put to good use. Even so, it was a remarkable achievement on the part of the great Swiss master Marc Birkigt to produce for the Paris Salon of 1919 what is, arguably, the greatest car of all time. This, the 37.2hp Hispano-Suiza, astonished everyone by its sheer magnificence. The engine was developed from the famous Hispano aero engines which had given French aviators the edge over their German opponents, and it was a masterpiece of mechanical engineering. Colonel Buckley in his *Cars of the Connoisseur* wrote in 1960: 'This lovely big 6-cylinder engine was unquestionably years ahead of its time. Like its aircraft forebear, it also was constructed almost entirely of light alloys ... The complete upper half of this most beautifully finished motor-car engine was rendered corrosion-proof by a closely guarded and patented process of enamelling under pressure. It was one of the finest examples of precision engineering ever made in the field of automobile manufacture ... Features of the design would be considered advanced today, though in this day and age the cost of producing such a motor car would be absolutely prohibitive, but to give some small idea of the standards of workmanship which went into it, the massive circular seven-main bearing crankshaft was machined and polished all over; it was machined from a solid billet of the very finest steel procurable, weighing in the rough 770 lb. The finished shaft – and finished it was to a jeweller's degree of accuracy – weighed 99 lb. A mere detail if you please but 671 lb of the finest steels available was machined away to produce this perfect shaft.'

All this *and* it was so easy to drive. According to the instruction book: 'The most perfect way of starting up on the level is to drive off on the second speed, practically without any gas admission. As soon as you feel that your car "is moving" shift the lever to the direct drive position and make no further change of gear, except in an emergency.'

With a top speed of up to 80mph, despite a body weight exceeding 2 tons, and for the first time reasonably effective servo-assisted brakes to all four wheels, it is hardly surprising that this was the car of which everyone dreamed but only the lucky ones – kings, maharajahs, millionaires and film stars – could own.

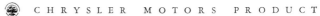

CHRYSLER "75" ROYAL SEDAN (*wire wheels extra*), $1535

Many a Roman aqueduct still stands, after 2000 years, the epitome of strength and beauty. That same charm of line and that same trustworthiness of construction are reflected in the "arched-window" silhouette of the Chrysler today.

A Wealth of Strength
Beneath Its Classic Beauty

WHEN the first Chrysler overthrew traditions of motor car beauty and behavior, there was a twofold purpose for devising the new practices in design and construction it introduced.

Chrysler engineers determined to replace awkward bulk with lithe grace, stodginess with alert and zestful performance. Guided by the canons of classic art, they translated authentic principles of beauty into automotive terms.

The purpose of Chrysler's new design was also to enhance the utility of the Chrysler car. The sturdy arches of the Roman aqueducts which have stood for 2000 years have been recognized as among the finest achievements of man's handiwork.

Not appearance alone directed Chrysler engineers to the arch of the aqueduct. The true arch is the acme of strength and rigidity, and so it was the Roman arch that served as the model for the construction of Chrysler windows and doors. Thus solidity and trustworthiness were concentrated at this point, masked by classic curve and flowing line.

It was not haphazard experiment and accidental achievement that developed Chrysler cars into symbols of grace in motion. They give greater value in performance as well as appearance because Chrysler engineers have never relinquished that twofold purpose of combining beauty with utility, swiftness with sturdiness, and luxury with dependability, in the proved integrity of Chrysler cars.

ℐ   ℐ   ℐ

New Chrysler "75" — *Nine body styles priced from $1535 to $2345. New Chrysler "65"—Six body styles priced from $1040 to $1145. Wire wheels extra. All prices f.o.b. factory.*

150

With slight modifications, the 37.2 Hispano was to retain its worldwide appeal into the mid-1930s. It was remarkably versatile, being driven with success in races and, more suitably, timed rallies. These events were usually followed by a *concours d'élégance* in which, adorned with a beautiful passenger, the car was carefully judged. Montague Grahame-White, one of the few Englishmen who, preferring presentation to performance, complained of the lack of creativity in English coachbuilders, managed to coax a beautiful *faux cabriolet* from Hoopers, to gain the highest award two years running at Cannes and win the first English *concours* at Southport in 1928. At Eastbourne that year his pleasure was increased by the company of the stage star José Collins in one of the new 8-cylinder models, the acceleration of which gave him the 'impression of standing in front of the hydraulically-opened ram attached to a 15-inch Naval gun'.

Birkigt's last great car, the 75hp V12, had such a beautiful engine that one owner specified glass windows to his bonnet tops so that it was there for all to see. At £3,750, only the defunct Bugatti Royale and the Model-J Duesenberg were more expensive; it was hardly a best seller but there was much sorrow when the great French factory at Bois Colombes went back to aero-engine manufacture just before the Second World War.

The Hispano caught the imagination of the fiction writer more than any other car and *La Cigogne Volante*, the mascot of French air ace Georges Guynemer on the car's magnificent bonnet was the final touch. Michael Arlen in *The Green Hat* wrote: 'Open as a yacht, it wore a great shining bonnet; and flying over the crest of this great bonnet, as though in proud flight over the heads of scores of phantom horses, was that silver stork by which the gentle may be pleased to know that they have just escaped death beneath the wheels of a Hispano-Suiza car, as supplied to His Most Catholic Majesty.'

The twenties were the era of great cars which had double-barrelled names – Isotta-Fraschini, Rolls-Royce, Mercedes-Benz – but Hispano-Suiza alone owed the combination to its origin, a Swiss engineer working in Spain. Although the fame of the early Hispanos spread when the Spanish king bought three at the 1905 Madrid Show, and a subsequent model came to be known as the Alfonso XIII, Birkigt moved to France, there to develop his finest engines. The Barcelona factory was retained to test his latest designs during the First World War but the new post-war model was put into production at Bois Colombes, leaving the Spanish end to continue manufacture of the 4-cylinder car.

Less fortunate was Ettore Bugatti, French by adoption, whose factory at Molsheim took several years to rise from the ashes of war before again producing cars which made *bugattisme* a cult. Difficult to start, their maker insisting on a heated garage, and renowned for their noise, the touring Bugattis followed closely the models which had won thousands of races and appealed strongly to young blades seeking character as well as speed.

Bugatti himself was quite a joker: he had one shot at producing a car for kings when, in 1927, the Type 41 Royale, with its white elephant ornament on the radiator, appeared on the market at a price of £5,250 for the chassis alone. Admittedly, the chassis boasted a wheelbase of 169 inches and the track 66, the same as a London bus, while the 8-cylinder engine gave a capacity of 12,760cc and produced 300bhp at the maximum permitted rpm of 2,000. Only seven Royales appeared on the roads but such enormity appealed to maharajahs and it is rumoured that parts shipped out but never assembled are still turning up in Indian palaces.

In 1929 Bugatti produced a more practical, scaled-down version of the monster with Type 46, a popular rich man's touring car. Ken W Purdy points out that 'to do business with *le patron* of Molsheim was made to feel an honour. When a driver had made a notable win against heavy odds, he might be given a Bugatti wristwatch. Even a customer might be given one if he were a notably *good* customer, say one who had bought eight or nine cars, and made no complaint of some little thing that went wrong with a couple of them.'

A very different French car competing for the grand market was the Renault. The post-war 45 was a stately Edwardian carriage which needed a coachman: it appealed to the elderly French whose dignity was enhanced by its sober black demeanour. In 1919 it was the world's largest car with an engine capacity of 9,123cc and a petrol consumption of eight miles per gallon. Later models included another heavyweight, the 8-cylinder Reina, favoured by the president of France.

The French car world never lacked personalities and Gabriel Voisin was one of the most brilliant. Tired of making aircraft he turned to cars after the First World War and his 'streamlined tanks' with their Knight double-sleeve-valve engines were a taste acquired over the years by a strange assortment of names from the Queen of Rumania and the Bey of Tunis to Rudolf Valentino, the owner of four. Another car with a sleeve-valve engine but lacking flamboyance, despite the goddess Athene which graced its bonnet, was the Belgian Minerva. Although well made and good value it failed to stir the imagination when compared to the Hispano-Suiza. Even so, by 1928 the English advertisers could boast an imposing number of royal patrons and successes at *concours d'élégance*, as well as victory in the Coupé des Alpes, the world's greatest reliability trial. Here the star turn was the 1928 Minerva 6-cylinder 32-4hp AK five-seater drop-head coupé, with coachwork by Carrosserie Vanden Plas of Brussels, priced at £1,650. This car deserved its considerable success in England, where the chassis was well treated by other top coachmakers, though Americans preferred bodies built in Paris by Howard Darrin.

Eastern potentates swelled the ranks of customers for the Speed Six which appeared in 1930 but, unfortunately, there were not enough exotic people to compensate for the small number of owners able to cope with a sleeve-valve engine. By the early 1930s, the Depression having heralded a reduction in the number of chauffeurs, motoring was

Freedom, if not exactly luxury: two young English gentlemen of 1922 in their much-cherished Bugatti tourer head gingerly up a country lane towards the open road.

becoming a pleasure for many more owner-drivers. The new Rolls-Bentley or, at a humbler level, mass-produced cars like the 25hp Vauxhall were proving much to their taste.

The Italian Isotta-Fraschini, product of a country with a small home market, was the marque which, in the early 1920s, competed most successfully with the Hispano-Suiza. The *tipo* 8 of 1919 offered a magnificent chassis, simultaneous braking to all four wheels and a 35.8hp engine which by 1925, in the Spinto, was increased in power to out-distance its rival.

Raymond Chandler called it 'an open phaeton, huge even for the calculated swank of Hollywood. It glittered like a Ziegfeld chorus as it passed the entrance lights, then it was dull grey and silver. A liveried chauffeur sat behind the wheel as stiff as a poker, with a peaked cap cocked rakishly over one eye. Rhonda Farr sat in the back seat, under the half-deck, with the rigid stillness of a wax figure.' No wonder it sold well in Hollywood: Jack Dempsey, Douglas Fairbanks, Ramon Novarro, Mary Pickford and Rudolf Valentino were among its owners. The great days of the Isotta-Fraschini were, undoubtedly, the late 1920s when 'the coupés, cabriolets and town cars of Castagna and Sala were things of beauty', and 8A landaulettes sold in America for nearly six times the price of a Packard.

From 1919 to 1930, the 'vintage' period of cars, the luxury motor carriage was very much in the image of the coach and horse; and, indeed, it was only towards the end of the 1920s that engines outnumbered horses on European roads. It was, accordingly, quite natural to choose an engine-chassis as you would choose a horse; and it was then up to your favourite coachbuilder to offer the carriage best suited to your needs. One English gentleman went so far as to have a lavatory installed in his otherwise elegant Renault.

These were the days when any car lover knew the difference between the various body types: berline, brougham, cabriolet, coupé de ville, fixed-head coupé, three-quarters coupé, gran turismo coupé, landaulette, sedan and tonneau. Preferences were legion. One point of view, expressed in the *Saturday Book 32*, was that 'apart from the enclosed limousine with division between chauffeur and passengers, there were two popular body styles on expensive chassis ... One was the landaulette, in which the rear portion of the roof folded down to give fresh air in fine weather, the ideal car in which to be seen in the park ... The other body style, more popular in Paris than in London, was the *sedanca de ville*, in which the chauffeur sat in the open, ahead of a limousine or landaulette style of passenger compartment.' Luxury cars with coachbuilt bodies could cost twice as much as the same chassis with a standard body and might take up to six months to complete. In 1920 the people behind the Minerva, one of

the first firms to offer a complete luxury car, found a strong demand but one which came mainly from hire-car operators. This was a mixed blessing, as it gave the car a poor image. Besides, the leading coachmakers were offering the most tempting variety of fittings: the buyer could choose carpets, curtains and woodwork, as well as chairs, tables and cocktail cabinets, as though for a living-room.

Cars were at their most elegant towards the end of the 1920s when Europe had caught the American fashion for matching colour schemes; and with European cars built to last, the antique dealer who chose *petit point* for his upholstery was anticipating many years of enjoyment. More muscular but no less bizarre was the tiger-hunting two-seater Mercedes S built for the Maharajah of Bhopal. The car had three spotlights, one on either side of the windscreen and the third on a collapsible frame that rose from a hidden recess behind the seats. It also had streamlined boxes above the running boards to carry hunting rifles. It may not have had the elevation and long-range view of a *howdah* but it was faster than any elephant: even so, there is no history of success by the Maharajah at dispensing death from his car's luxurious seats.

In the London Motor Show of 1928 the Rolls-Royce was shown on its own stand fitted with coachwork by Barkers, Thrupp and Maberley, and Windovers as well as on the stands of twelve other English coachmakers. Motoring correspondents showed scant respect to the ladies who were said 'to be anxious to try the cushions and comfort of the seating whenever the opportunity occurs' and to be in favour of the car with the prettiest colour scheme.

French automotive couturiers, naturally, had an eye for the chic, and such names as Falaschi, Letournier et Marchand and Saoutchik were responsible for some of the more original winners of the *concours d'élégance*. Some buyers were tempted to choose car colours to suit the costume of the passengers but Chanel, the great designer, did not appreciate this new fad: 'She bought a car, a dark blue Rolls upholstered in black leather. "You don't think it's too funereal?" they asked in the showrooms. It was the era of bad taste: people often had their cars upholstered in *toile de Jouy*, or watered silk, or lace!' And there were German firms which specialized in formal carosserie, Hermann Spöhn and Gläser of Dresden being among the best known.

In the early post-war years, the height of ambition for most car buyers must have been the open tourer, high off the ground, with artillery-type wheels; and at the London Motor Show of 1919 these looked positively jolly alongside the rather gloomy closed bodies of cars like the 40hp Lanchester. American cars all had much the same look but were attractive to those wanting high horse power at a low price. Even after adding the *ad valorem* tax of 33 per cent, introduced in 1915 to protect the home market, the Chevrolet 22hp sold in England for as little as £260, about half the cost of its European counterpart.

If the typical post-war car lacked glamour, the manufacturers made the most of the romance of motoring.

A view (right) of the London Motor Show in 1928. A star of this exhibition and, indeed, for years one of the world's most-coveted cars was the Rolls-Royce, a coupé de ville version of which is seen here (above) at Le Touquet, France, at about that time.

The *Illustrated London News* of June 1919 carried the following advertisement for the 20hp Austin: 'The many-tinted magician may fill the sky with the glorious cascade of colour and the evening air may be cool and sweet scented as Ambrosia – but nothing short of motoring efficiency will enable the traveller to enjoy Nature's charm to the full. On an "Austin Twenty" he is secure from most of the worries and anxieties which too often disturb a roadman's holiday, and after a delightful spin over hill and dale arrives without mishap – at the end of a perfect day.'

This depicted motoring in ideal conditions. Had the heading been 'Twenty Degrees of Frost' instead of 'Sunset', the picture would have been rather less enticing, for not even the beautiful Hispano could boast a heater. Motorists were obliged to dress up against the elements as their forebears had done in the days of the horse and cart, which was still the standard conveyance for most Europeans.

Whereas the car was accepted in America as a blessing there was considerable opposition to it in other countries. The conservative Swiss gained a reputation for being handy with their stones and some cantons closed their roads to the motorist on Sundays. The roads in Europe were generally adequate for the prevailing traffic though the quality varied: for example, the *routes nationales* of

France were straighter than the trunk roads of England. The obstacles were not all physical. In England a reactionary element had delayed the introduction of the car at the beginning of the century by means of ridiculously low speed-limits. It was a triumph in 1903 when the limit was raised from 14 to 20mph, the latter remaining nominally in force until 1930. Furthermore, class envy made itself felt to the extent that motorists were advised to keep a low profile in certain industrial areas.

In those days intelligent people, among whom every aspiring motorist counted himself, tended to believe at the outset that learning to drive would present no problem. W A McKenzie confesses to driving his first car for some time before discovering the object of the clutch. Whenever he slowed down, the engine stalled; and it was no sinecure restarting a hot engine – with some engines it was better to let them first cool off. Fortunately, the camaraderie of the road being strong, there was always a fellow motorist

Opposite: Le Renault might hold its own in the 1920s with the Arc de Triomphe, but for all its Gallic character it was no match for the Hispanos and Isotta-Fraschinis.

Lucky fellow! A fine car, three lovely ladies and, guess what: the latest in 'portable' wireless sets, with horn to help get the music past those hats.

Those tiresome punctures! In the 1920s hardly a journey was
completed without one and it was fortunate that the camaraderie of the
road was strong, especially for the *demoiselle* in distress.

willing to stop and give a push.

The Dornford Yates character Berry, after only three driving lessons, declared: 'I insist upon plain English. I'm not going to be suddenly yelled at to "double-clutch", or "feel the brake", or "close the throttle" or something. It makes me want to burst into tears. That fellow who was teaching me asked me, without any warning and in the middle of some sheep, what I should do if one of my "big ends were to run out". I said I should consult a specialist, but the question upset me. Indirectly it also upset the shepherd ... Which reminds me, I never knew a human being could jump so far. The moment he felt the radiator...'

Two very different cars stood out in the twenties among the higher-priced British species, the Rolls-Royce and the Bentley. Both were superbly engineered, the products of total dedication by their creators, Frederick Henry Royce and W O Bentley respectively. But while the Rolls, with its appeal to VIPs, seemed to demand a chauffeur to go with it (and one early model actually housed a throne for an Indian prince, with seats for four attendants in front), the Bentley appealed more to the dashing young men who believed there was no better car than a good British car.

Bentley's first model appeared in 1919 at the London Motor Show and, like the Hispano, incorporated much that had been learned from the development of aero engines during the war. This 3-litre model was beautifully engineered and, although few were available before 1921, its popularity was such that 1,639 were sold in six years at a chassis price of some £1,000. Cecil Clutton and John Stanford in *The Vintage Motor Car* wrote: 'Although the 3-litre Bentley is now looked upon as quite a large car, it was thought of in 1920 as the smallest sort of machine from which real performance could be obtained in conjunction with tolerably comfortable four-seater coachwork ... It represented a very real advance towards the typical Vintage sports car, with its well designed electrical equipment, high-speed, high-efficiency engine, and close-ratio gearbox ... Bentley only claimed a 75 mph maximum for his 3-litre, but a sustained cruising speed of 65 mph from a 3-litre production car in 1920 was an entirely novel proposition. Long mileages between overhauls and low petrol consumption (30 mpg at 30 mph) were other features justly claimed for the Bentley, which did so much to put England on the map by its Le Mans successes and thus greatly enhanced the prestige of English cars on the Continent.'

Almost regretfully, Bentley went on to make more powerful cars. He has since explained that 'as soon as you had produced a car that became liked, the customer began to demand more – more body, more silence, more performance ... Now the 3-litre was never intended to carry closed coachwork at all, and much of the charm that it possessed began to disappear when you did so. Closed bodies were very heavy, so some of the performance was lost ... This resulted in disappointment and a demand for something bigger. So up went the engine to $4\frac{1}{2}$ litres, and the same thing happened again; ... and so was born the Big

Six, of $6\frac{1}{2}$ litres. This was quite as fast, and a great deal more refined than the 4-cylinder cars. Inevitably, in time though, seven-seater coachwork found its way on to this chassis, performance fell, and gentlemen who had bought a Bentley in part because of its reputation for reliability *and* speed were disappointed.' Then, 'it is my experience that everybody in the end wants silence in a motor car. This is what we intended to give them with the next car. We also aimed at giving those who prized such a luxury a 100 mph motor car that would carry seven people in complete silence and security.' It was an impressive experience to start the 8-litre, put it in top gear, and then walk beside it without hearing a sound.

Bentley made about a hundred 8-litre cars before the financial troubles of 1931 when the company was taken over by Rolls-Royce. This 8-litre was a truly magnificent, fast machine, and it presented a threat to Rolls-Royce which hitherto had dominated this market with its Phantom.

The rivalry with Rolls had become apparent when the Bentley factory was experimenting with the prototype of a $4\frac{1}{2}$-litre 6-cylinder and, having fitted the chassis with an uncharacteristically ugly sedan body as disguise, took the car for testing in France. 'They were rapidly approaching a Y-junction as another strange-looking and unrecognisable car raced for the junction on the other leg. Neither of them gave way and both cars flew into the stem of the Y side by side. Both parties immediately saw through the camouflage. The other car was the new Phantom I Rolls-Royce, also on test. Both drivers stamped on their accelerators and roared along side by side, filling the narrow tree-lined *route nationale*, neither managing to beat the other ... They'd very likely have run right on into the English Channel had not the cap of one of the Rolls Royce passengers blown off. The Rolls stopped to retrieve it and the Bentley went on.' After that Bentley decided to increase the power of his car from $4\frac{1}{2}$ to $6\frac{1}{2}$ litres to be sure of being a lap ahead of his rival.

The Bentley gained many converts in the twenties but the Rolls was already an established religion. The magnificent Silver Ghost, so far ahead when it appeared in 1907 that it long held its place as the best car in the world, was still in production. Compared to the Hispano-Suiza its image was now somewhat dowdy but the English motoring press found it almost sacrilege to do more than whisper that the Derby works might, conceivably, be resting on its laurels. For the Silver Ghost (or the 40/50, as it was often known) belonged with the gods. The car was so quiet on the road that the horn had to be used, as though bestowing a favour, to advise pedestrians of its approach. It was so well made as to be almost indestructible, and it could proceed in top gear at a stately walking pace or hurry elegantly at 70mph if the roads were straight enough for long enough. It was accepted by the faithful that changes would not be made until innovations had been thoroughly tested. Thus, four-wheel brakes were not introduced until 1924; and the long-awaited new model, the Phantom, did not appear until the following year.

Meanwhile a 'baby' Rolls, the Twenty, was introduced

in October 1922, its 20hp 6-cylinder chassis costing £1,100. It was not very fast but from this model developed the pre-war Rolls-Bentley and the Wraith. The *Autocar* reports how a journey made in the Twenty from London to Glasgow in 1923 was completed in two days 'without fatigue': 'We set out along the Great North Road ... creeping stealthily through Barnet in top gear. Once clear of traffic we sped along the tarmac road surface with a fleetness and a silence only impaired by the hiss of the tyres on the hard highway and the tick tick – yes, remarkable though it may seem! – of the speedometer mechanism.'

The Rolls of this period was offered by high-class English coachmakers with an enormous variety of detail.

As a precaution against running out of fuel on long runs in its home country, some owners fitted a row of two-gallon petrol tins at the rear. This was vital as petrol pumps were introduced only from 1920 as the result of an Automobile Association official visiting America and finding, to his surprise, that the red can was not the only possible source of petrol. Other rear tanks were designed especially to accommodate dogs, indispensable adjunct of shooting parties, or golf clubs, a popular choice after the Prince of Wales had his new 40-50hp Phantom so equipped in 1928. The latter, incidentally, was a Weymann saloon, built under licence by Gurney Nutting; it had a type of wooden body covered with a fabric to minimize the squeaks.

In 1932 a rather more exciting version of the Phantom II appeared, the Continental 40-50hp. Here was a Rolls with enough speed to live with the 8-litre Bentley, its 6-cylinder engine of 7,669cc developing remarkable acceleration. Business was hard to get following the Depression and competition from the V12 Hispano-Suiza, the J Duesenberg and upstarts like the Cadillac V16 so strong that, for the first time, Rolls made the Phantom available with a standard body; and it was even possible to have left-hand steering. Meanwhile, the Rolls-Royce operation in Springfield, Massachusetts, had been closed down, leaving the American market to be supplied exclusively from Derby.

When Rolls-Royce took over the Bentley marque in 1931, it did so to eliminate a competitor rather than acquire the services of W O Bentley who, before long, joined Lagonda and created their V12. However, the Lagonda was unable to reach its peak before the outbreak of the Second World War. The Rolls-Bentley which appeared in 1933 bore little relation to W O's last design, the grand 8-litre of 1930 which was killed by the Depression, but it was an intelligent response to the demand for a comfortable and fast car. The dashing young men of the twenties, having enjoyed their Bentley bone-shakers, were now ready to chauffeur their families in the more luxurious 3½-litre (increased to 4½ in 1936) 'Silent Sports Car'. Costs were

One of a long line of thoroughbred racing cars which first made their mark in the 1920s, this 4½-litre Bentley shows its paces on a tough road in hilly country.

A 1932 picture of a Stutz Super Bearcat convertible. After Duesenberg, Stutz with its 'rakish, aggressive styles' was perhaps the most glamorous name in the American galaxy of motoring giants.

kept down by sharing many components with the baby Rolls. The car gained a faithful following of Britons who wanted the best but, through a strange inverted snobbery, did not wish to own a Rolls, overt symbol of the rich.

Abroad, of course, attitudes were different: the Rolls was a symbol of status, a distinct attribute which, evidently, attracted bouquets more than brickbats. However, the rather ambivalent British view was well expressed in the book *Viscount Lee of Fareham*: 'Sir George Lloyd, High Commissioner in Cairo in 1926, drove Ruth Lee in an open Rolls-Royce at breakneck speed on the road back to Cairo from Heliopolis explaining that he always drove at 70mph as it lessened the risk of assassination. Previously he had driven Arthur Lee through one of Bombay's disturbed quarters with light on and coat open to expose decorations so there could be no possible doubt as to *who* he was if anyone wished to shoot.'

In 1935 came the Phantom III which remained the Rolls standard bearer until after the Second World War. Its magnificent 12-cylinder V engine of 7.3 litres capacity caused the *Autocar* to run out of hyperboles in explaining it to mere mortals, few of whom could hope to enter its hallowed doors. Nearing 3 tons laden and costing upwards of £2,500, this touring limousine 'floated' along at up to 90mph, somewhat thirstily averaging 10mpg. It was a fine example of the work of British engineers, more self-effacing than the French who produced many overtly elegant but tiring-to-drive cars, and totally different from the powerful German steeds which needed really strong drivers, as befitted the *Herrenvolk*. It called for a high order of craftsmanship, not to mention design, to create not merely three of the best-selling luxury cars but to develop the Merlin aero engine which did so much to save Britain from being overwhelmed by the Luftwaffe in 1940.

Many advertisements of British luxury cars in the vintage era stressed the qualities of effortless motion, silence and docility. A telling portrayal was that of smartly dressed chauffeurs walking alongside their carriages, engines in top gear, final proof of their machines'

The silently immaculate Rolls-Royce Phantom I, worthy successor to the famous Silver Ghost, was a top car of the 1920s, a period when top people were beginning to be choosy.

impeccable breeding. In these respects, despite growing legends to the contrary, Rolls did not have it all their way for the 1920s saw the development of the sleeve-valve engine invented by Charles Yale Knight. This was quieter and less thirsty than the ordinary engine and was adopted not only by Packard, Voisin and Minerva but also by Daimler. The latter's ponderous cars, with a cruising speed of 45mph, gave way in 1926 to their Double-Six with its top speed of 80mph. The success of the Daimler was largely due to King George V to whose sedate image they were admirably suited. It would have pleased him that over one thousand Daimlers were earmarked to convey the dignitaries attending the expected coronation of his son Edward VIII, even though the new monarch himself had a penchant for Buicks which, to appease the trade unions, were imported from Canada.

As Prince of Wales, Edward had been obliged to fight for his right to drive. George V had written with heavy paternal heart: 'I must beg of you not to drive fast and to be most careful when you are driving, it makes both Mama and me most anxious, as any little mistake and the accident occurs. I must confess I do not approve of your driving a motor ... It is impossible for you to drive as well as an expert who does it every day of his life and you must remember your position and who you are, and that the slightest accident that you have would be exaggerated and in every paper in Europe.'

Whatever cars the British Royal Family preferred for their private use, for State occasions they long remained faithful to the Daimler. When George V died in 1935 no less than ten were in service, five of them for his own use: a brougham, a State limousine for Queen Mary, a private car and two for the household. All were made especially high to allow room for bearskins or other lofty headgear.

Such considerations of formal dress added an extra complication to royal specifications, as the makers of the Talbot discovered to their dismay. The Talbot was one of a splendid line of sports cars developed by George Roesch which proved themselves in handicap racing and at Le Mans. However, the English factory was let down by the complicated finances of the Sunbeam–Talbot–Darracq combine, and after 1935 English Talbots were to be submerged in the relative mediocrity of the Rootes empire.

In the 1932 Motor Show, the Talbot 105 Tourer was the fastest British car, with a top speed of 95mph. The Duke of Kent was impressed enough to order one in Vanden Plas Saloon form to replace his Bentley. News of this sale set the seal on the prestige of the Talbot factory, establishing it as the foremost sports-car manufacturer in the land. Every care having been lavished upon the car's manufacture, it was delivered in person by three directors, top hats in hand.

Their reception at Buckingham Palace by a royal chauffeur, instead of the Duke in person, was an anti-climax. But worse was to follow. Three days later they were summoned to the Mews to hear of the car's shortcomings. It transpired that 'every Royal car had to be so constructed that its occupants could travel comfortably within, under the shelter of their official top hats; and it further appeared that when Prince George had taken his first ride in the car, protocol had nearly obliged him to sit upon the floor. There was a small matter of four extra inches of headroom to be arranged inside the low-built Talbot body ... They were duly found, but only by raising the windscreen and roofline.'

The much-loved Vauxhall was an earlier take-over casualty, having been absorbed by General Motors in 1926. The E-type 30/98 (in 1923, the OE 30/98), basically an Edwardian car, suited the young English sportsmen of the twenties and had nearly as many *aficionados* as the Bentley. The instruction book was honest: 'Should it become necessary to check the car's progress, the handbrake is the correct brake to use, the foot-operated brake being in reserve for emergency.' This car's lack of braking power

was notorious, but for speed and road-holding it was splendid.

A Vauxhall could do much for its driver's ego, as Aldous Huxley recounts in *Those Barren Leaves*: 'Lord Hovendon detached from his motor car was an entirely different being from the Lord Hovendon who lounged with such a deceptive air of languor behind the steering wheel of a Vauxhall Velox. Half an hour spent in the roaring wind of his own speed transformed him from a shy and diffident boy into a cool-headed hero ... The fierce wind blew away his diffidence; the speed intoxicated him out of his self-consciousness. All his victories had been won while he was in the car. It was in the car ... that he had ventured to ask his guardian to increase his allowance; and he had driven faster and faster until, in sheer terror, his guardian had agreed ... It was on board the Velox that he had ventured to tell Mrs Terebruth, who was seventeen years older than he, had four children and adored her husband, that she was the most beautiful woman he had ever seen ... When she laughed and told him he was an impudent young shrimp, he felt not a whit abashed, but laughed back, pressed the accelerator down a little further, and when the needle of the speedometer touched eighty, shouted through the wind and the noise of the engine: "But I love you."'

With good roads, great engineers and plentiful finance, it had come naturally to France to be the home of motor racing—and even before the First World War their Grand Prix was *the* Grand Prix. When this race was resumed in 1921 there began a series remarkable for the lack of competition, the race tending to become a platform for the outstanding car of the moment. The capacity selected in this first year was 3 litres, applicable also to races at Indianapolis, and overall the Duesenberg was the most successful car. In 1924 the British had their one triumph with the Sunbeam but thereafter were outclassed by the French, Italians and Germans, each enjoying their period of success. Constant changes were made in the car formulas and, in 1936, when it became obvious under the prevailing rules that the Delage and Bugatti (Type 59) could not hope to compete with the increased power of the German models, the French turned the whole event over to sports cars, in which they could excel with appropriate types of Bugatti and Delahaye.

Second to France in road-racing events came Italy with

The great racing drivers Tazio Nuvolari (opposite), the 'Flying
Mantuan', at the wheel of an Alfa Romeo on the last lap of the Monaco
Grand Prix of 1931, and (below) Rudolf Caracciola at a pit stop with
his Mercedes-Benz during his victorious drive in the 1931 German
Grand Prix.

the Coppa, the Targa Florio, the Italian Grand Prix
(inaugurated in 1912) and the Mille Miglia, which covered
a thousand miles of public roads, from Brescia via Rome
and back to Brescia. W F Bradley in the *Autocar* described
how, in 1930, 'running over level dusty roads, often with a
stream of water on each side, the competitors made their
way through village after village, with the natives safely
ensconced in doorways, at windows, on ledges, in the trees
or, occasionally in the more important centres, behind a
rope or protected by a flimsy hoarding'. And Anthony
Pritchard tells of Mussolini's support for a race which
'would demonstrate the toughness and virility of the Italian
nation' and which the home team, knowing the road,
would, with reasonable luck, win.

Mussolini was the first dictator to appreciate the national
prestige to be gained by a successful racing team, and the
drivers of the Alfa Romeos became the heroes of the second
Roman Empire. In 1930 the greatest of them all, Tazio
Nuvolari, 'The Flying Mantuan', joined the Scuderia
Ferrari team of Alfa drivers. The next year it was
Nuvolari's driving that won the team both the Targa Florio
and the Italian Grand Prix. In 1935, after an interval of two
years with Maseratis, he was persuaded to return to the

Scuderia Ferrari in order to stem the tide of German
victories. In the German Grand Prix at Nürburgring,
driving a new 3.8-litre version of the Alfa Monoposto, he
won a thrilling victory over von Brauchitsch's Mercedes.
But his finest hour was in 1936, when he scored four
victories over the new, vastly superior German cars,
driving at Livorno 'at almost maniacal speed, slashing
seconds off the leader's advantage on every lap, gaining
time at every corner by his unique technique of
approaching the corner too fast, deliberately to encourage a
slide, and with a quiet flick of the wheel using that slide
both to slow the car and set it up for the exit from the
corner'.

The Germans were not a force in the motoring world for
some years after the First World War, but once they
returned to racing their progress was unparalleled. In the
1930s they would have swept the board in *les grandes
épreuves* had it not been for the Alfas. Their cars were
brutes to drive, heavy and bad road-holders, but nothing
was allowed to stand in the way of their success, even if this
needed the help of foreign drivers. When the Auto-Union
star Bernard Rosemeyer was killed during a record
attempt, Nuvolari was persuaded to sign for them. Already

Above: The German Maybach firm, leading makers of airship and airplane engines, also built high-quality luxury cars: a 1936 view of the 5.2-litre 6-cylinder Type DSH.

Right: Daimler, later to join forces with Benz, was long one of the most respected names in motor car history: a 1900 view of one of the earliest production-controlled assembly plants.

in his late forties, Nuvolari had hardly accustomed himself to the heavy Auto-Unions when war broke out. His first and final victory for them in Grand Prix racing was on the day France declared war with Germany; von Brauchitsch in a Mercedes-Benz was runner-up.

One of the German achievements was Maybach's 12-cylinder Zeppelin which Lord Montagu describes as the 'recognised carriage of the Teuton Elite'. The fastest European car in its class and engineered with great precision, it was cheaper than the Rolls and Duesenberg. However, its handicap of being a heavyweight Hun was too much to attract the French and English unless they had a fetish about gearboxes, the Zeppelin boasting the *Doppelschnellgang* with eight forward speeds and two reverse. The marque gained some useful publicity when a $3\frac{1}{2}$-litre SW-35 was presented to Prince Bernhard on his marriage to Princess Juliana of the Netherlands.

Before the First World War German cars were successful in Swedish winter races. None had done better than the Horch, and this marque continued to have a following in Sweden. In the 1930s the straight-eight Horch convertible was fashionable among the Swedish smart set and this product of the firm was considered a vastly improved car, with some of the Zeppelin's elegance, at less than half its price.

The brilliant but perverse Dr Porsche not only designed the winning Auto-Union Grand Prix cars but had earlier been responsible for the Mercedes-Benz which, in 1927, after Daimler and Benz had joined forces, was aimed at

sports-car events. The heavy K, Porsche's first car for his new company, was soon succeeded by the S or 36-220 Mercedes, a superb sports car, famed for its supercharger. It was to find an outstanding driver in Rudi Caracciola.

According to Ralph Stein in *The Great Cars*: 'A Rootes-type, it blew through the two Pallas carburetors, causing that beloved, ear-assaulting, scalp-lifting Mercedes scream, not unlike that of a lighthouse diaphone at close quarters. Other blowers on lesser cars were not quite so decibel-making since they sucked mixture from their carburetors before pumping it into the cylinders. Further, the blowers on other cars were spinning all the time. A Mercedes-Benz blower worked only when you wanted extra effort from the engine and tramped hard on the loud pedal. At that foot-on-the-floor instant a clutch engaged the supercharger. The factory discouraged over-enthusiasm with the blower. No more than twenty seconds while accelerating, and never in low gear nor in high at top speed, were the suggested limitations on use lest the engine be debilitated. I doubt, however, the lovely tale that

continual use of the supercharger could cause the engine to macerate itself into bits small enough to exit through the exhaust system.'

Before the restless Porsche left Mercedes in 1928 to become in due course a freelance consultant, he had already produced a more powerful version with the ominous initials SS, as well as the SSK (K being for *kurtz* – short). The latter was produced with the help of Hans Nibel who took over future developments. Next came the SSKL (L for *leicht* – light) which, in the 1931 Grand Prix of

Nürburgring, beat even the larger formula Bugattis and Alfas. Anti-German feeling had not permitted German cars to appear at the London Motor Show before 1927, when Mercedes exhibited their 36-220 S. This was basically the machine driven by Caracciola, and the drophead coupé version with curling exhaust pipes outside the bonnet must have attracted even the most prejudiced eye.

No one did more for the motor car than Hitler. Following the example of Mussolini who built the first length of *autostrada* in 1925, Hitler's 7,000km of *Reichsautobahnen*, completed in the 1930s, were the envy of the world. To give mobility in war, the German nation was to be motorized and the omnipresent Dr Porsche was brought in to design the Volkswagen, a cheap car with low petrol consumption. The number of cars on German roads more than doubled between 1932 and 1937.

The Nazi chiefs enjoyed their motorcades. To visitors, especially for a Jew like Leonard Woolf, the scene could be a little unnerving. During a tour of Germany in 1935, on the way to Mainz with his wife Virginia and a pet marmoset Mitz, Woolf found himself directed down the presidential route, lined with enthusiastic crowds waiting to cheer Goering. The unexpected sight of Mitz on his master's shoulder in an open car caused shrieks of delight and loud shouts of *Heil Hitler! Heil Hitler!*

The Mercedes was the car which Hitler used almost as an extension of his own personality, his attachment dating from 1928 when he had been given a K model. When, later, he received the Aga Khan at Berchtesgarten, he offered him forty Mercedes in exchange for one of the Aga's racing horses. The Aga is said to have replied that he had no wish to set up as a salesman in Piccadilly. The 540K Mercedes and 7.7 Grosser Mercedes had by now become the cars for the Nazi bosses; lesser fry and the *Wehrmacht* had to be content with the Horch.

Hitler's vision was of a Mercedes truly worthy of the Third Reich and funds were provided in the early 1930s for production to go over to the Grand Prix car. Everything Mussolini did Hitler did better and, in the late 1930s, the Mercedes and Auto-Unions were busy thrashing the Italians in the heavier formula. Meantime, other Europeans, in their sports cars, were having far more light-hearted fun.

For the British, who had to overcome the initial handicap of being forbidden to race on their own public roads, the prestidigious event in the late twenties became the race at Le Mans. From 1923, this was the first event for catalogued cars. It was ideally suited to British taste and temperament, ingenuity and enterprise being as essential to success as access to somewhat limited funds. The dangers and delights of driving non-stop for twenty-four hours on a

A girl speeds in carefree 1930s mood along the Leipzig–Beyreuth stretch of a German autobahn, an early example of today's international networks of express motorways and highways.

ten-mile circuit caught the public imagination and victory brought much valued publicity to the successful marque. In the early years, strangely, more cars failed to finish through lamp than engine troubles: the night session was quite often a case of follow-my-leader, the leader being the lucky competitor with headlamps still working.

At first the British approach to Le Mans was lackadaisical, W O Bentley himself considering that his cars were not designed for twenty-four hours of consecutive running. But all this changed when one good performance by a privately-entered Bentley in 1924 was followed by two poor ones by factory-entered cars as a result of unnecessary faults. Here was a challenge and the Bentley works answered it with wins in 1927–30, before retiring from racing. Although 1929 was the Bentley works team's greatest year with the Speed Six winning at 73.62mph, just ahead of two 4½-litre cars, their last race was the most dramatic. Outpowered by the supercharged 38–250 Mercedes driven by Caracciola, the greatest racing driver apart from Nuvolari, the British won again through the teamwork of the now famous Bentley Boys.

While Bentley buyers read like 'an anthology of Debrett and the Directory of Directors' their drivers, too, included some rich young society men whose life of wine and women between wins became a legend. The most famous of them, Babe Barnato, son of the diamond millionaire, became the firm's chairman during its first financial crisis in 1926. It was he who won Le Mans in 1930 in a 6½-litre Bentley after Tim Birkin (Sir H S Birkin) in a supercharged 4½-litre had teased and tormented Caracciola in his 7½-litre Mercedes into constant use of the supercharger. Finally, at 4.30am, 'its scream died away' and 'the white teutonic menace' was out of the race. Although W O had detested superchargers for perverting the design of his engines, making them unreliable, this did not prevent an independently-financed trio of 4½-litre 'blown' Bentleys being raced by Birkin with considerable success.

Britain excelled in producing drivers, both gentlemen and professionals. In the early 1930s, when there were more successful British drivers than cars, they had to look abroad for machines. Dick Seaman scored many of his successes in a rebuilt 1926 Delage after finding the ERA unsatisfactory, while one of the greatest of the amateurs, Lord Howe (Viscount Curzon), settled for the ERA after displaying a penchant for Bugattis. He and Birkin had driven Alfa-Romeos to win in 1931 at Le Mans at the beginning of that marque's vintage period.

At home, short-distance competitions were the only ones possible within British road regulations before the Castle Donington circuit was opened in the 1930s. The track at Brooklands, 2¾ miles long and steeply banked, a real test of nerves, produced some exciting handicap racing, with cars lapping at record high speeds. In 1930

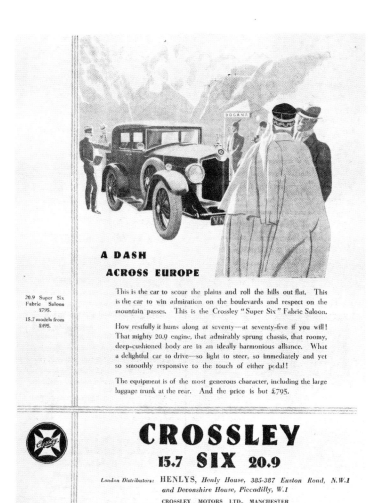

A DASH
ACROSS EUROPE

20.9 Super Six
Fabric Saloon
£795.

15.7 models from
£495.

This is the car to scour the plains and roll the hills out flat. This is the car to win admiration on the boulevards and respect on the mountain passes. This is the Crossley "Super Six" Fabric Saloon.

How restfully it hums along at seventy—at seventy-five if you will! That mighty 20.9 engine, that admirably sprung chassis, that roomy, deep-cushioned body are in an ideally harmonious alliance. What a delightful car to drive—so light to steer, so immediately and yet so smoothly responsive to the touch of either pedal!

The equipment is of the most generous character, including the large luggage trunk at the rear. And the price is but £795.

CROSSLEY
15.7 SIX 20.9

London Distributors: HENLYS, Henly House, 385-387 Euston Road, N.W.1 and Devonshire House, Piccadilly, W.1

CROSSLEY MOTORS LTD., MANCHESTER

The hills may not have been rolled out flat but this Crossley is certainly winning all due respects as it pauses for a customs check in a European mountain pass.

Opposite: A smart luxury sports car stars in this romantic 1927 advertisement of elaborately chic beachwear modelled by a gowned he-man with coquettes in playful attendance.

cars more than ten years old were supposedly banned but a 1913 21½-litre Benz lapped at 113mph while Delages, Bentleys and Sunbeams averaged over 130mph, John Cobb finally topping them all in his 24-litre Napier-Railton at 143.44mph. The *Autocar* had been far from alone when it complained that 'a more horrid spectacle has probably never been seen in motor racing' than Parry Thomas matched in his Leyland 8 against E A D Eldridge in a fiercesome, reconstituted Fiat nicknamed *Mephistopheles*, being down to the treads of their tyres by the tenth and final lap.

Another entertainment was the long-distance reliability trial, the London to Land's End run, including some Somerset hills which the spectators hoped would prove too much for the heavier small cars. One of the most enjoyable features was the standing start on a steep part of Porlock Hill which left the weakest stuck, while the progress of others was often so slow that drivers were seen to drop a handkerchief in order to judge accurately whether their cars were actually in motion.

The period from 1919 to 1929 is a long time in European motoring history. In Britain alone cars increased from over $\frac{1}{4}$ million to nearly $1\frac{1}{2}$ million, the greatest rise being in the number of small cars. France was second, with 1 million cars. It was estimated that there was one person to every 55.9 cars in Britain; in the USA, however, the ratio was 1:5.8.

During this period, the open tourer largely gave way to the closed saloon, with windscreen wiping posing one of the most intractable problems. For a while, a hand-operated wiper was one of the lamer answers. There were other snags, among them the 'dangers' of closed saloons, as pointed out by the motoring correspondent of the *Sketch*, Heniochus, in October 1928: 'One must stress the need for far greater care being taken by owners of closed saloons to see they are gas tight so as to prevent the exhaust fumes penetrating the interior ... The official view is they are more likely to develop as death traps unless due precautions are taken to ventilate them and seal the floors.'

But the worst temptation with the closed car was to create bodies too heavy for the engine. To improve stability, cars became lower, although they still retained running boards. Balloon tyres, which made riding more comfortable, became standard, even if they led to problems with punctures and wheel-wobble. Dame Freya Stark complained: 'I am in Persia for a week, invited by an old friend of ours, Eric Maxwell, who is in Baghdad as a judge and decided to bring his car up ... I hate cars, I decide more and more: all one's time is spent tinkering at the million things that go wrong with them, and everyone who has to do with them in the way of commerce becomes a criminal ... I am practising driving. It is fun, but not travel I consider – and barbarous to have to rush along with one's eye on the road all the time.'

As for the cost of becoming a motorist, the London Motor Show of 1928 provides some pointers. This exhibition included a tremendous variety of cars, although

The scene illustrated is the old George Inn at Huntingdon.

THE finest conceptions of craftsmanship, of line and of colour are embodied in every Morris Coupé. The skill of the artisan and his pride in his work are reflected in every curve of the commodious body and in every mechanical detail—beautiful to see. No other car gives such elegance, such dependability and such performance at so low a cost.

Morris Cowley Coupé £180 ; Morris Oxford Coupé £225 ; Morris Six Coupé £365

Dunlop Tyres Standard. Triplex at slight extra cost.

MORRIS

MORRIS MOTORS (1926) LTD., COWLEY, OXFORD

 BUY BRITISH AND BE PROUD OF IT

This 1914 British Mercury car was the kind of two-seater runabout coveted by some of the wealthy young people in the aftermath of the First World War.

A copy-writer's dream? This galaxy of Morris cars at an English country inn makes a point with éclat and a sense of excitement.

over half the British firms in business in 1922 had already given up. The price range for the popular 6-cylinder car was now £250 to £3,000. The Alvis, for example, came with a four-door saloon at £695, the Sunbeam range started at £550, while the Austin 20 Ranelagh limousine cost £595. At the other end of the price range, the 6-cylinder baby Rolls cost £1,185 for the chassis alone. On this occasion there were thirty-eight British car exhibits on view, twenty-three from France, six from Italy, three from Belgium, two from Germany and twenty-three from Canada and the USA.

Much of the glamour went out of motoring in the thirties. The earlier cars had very definite personalities and, long after their prime, the superior marques had a strange air of aloof gentility. Anthony Powell understood it well: 'The navy blue car was built high off the ground and the name on the bonnet recalled a bankrupt, forgotten firm of motor-makers. Inside, the car was done up in a material like grey corduroy, with folding seats in unexpected places, constructed liberally to accommodate some Edwardian Swiss Family Robinson. This was a period piece. An exhibit. The brakes had ceased to work long since. On the wall in front, immediately behind the chauffeur's neck, which was goose-flesh in spite of that heat, there was a German silver vase for flowers and below it a looking-glass, distorting but powerful.'

The ranks of chauffeurs, many of them former coachmen, became greatly reduced as money became

The self-starter in place of the heavy cranking handle brought to women the freedom of the road; and from that freedom followed the two-car family.

scarcer. In England many survived until the Second World War, not least with ducal families such as the Bedfords: 'Although Duke Herbrand (the 11th Duke) visited London barely once a year, he kept two fully staffed establishments in Belgrave Square and eight chauffeurs. A guest to Woburn would be taken in one car, with chauffeur and private footman, while his luggage would travel with its own chauffeur and footman in another car. On the outskirts of London, both cars would be met by two more sent from Woburn, and passenger and luggage would transfer from one vehicle to another.' Yet it is on record that when the Duchess, an intrepid aviator, by choice unaccompanied by a chauffeur, broke down in a narrow Devon lane, it was she who changed the wheel. None of the drivers of the cars who were held up by the puncture were capable of doing such a job on a Rolls.

1930 was, indeed, well chosen as the end of the vintage era in cars. Lord Montagu sums it up: 'After the Depression the concept of luxury motoring changed. Money was tight, and though the well-to-do were still prepared to pay £1,300 and more for a motor car, they could no longer afford something they would never think of driving themselves. Hence the emphasis on the *grand routier* and on 'touring limousine' styles suitable for both owner or chauffeur-drive. Such cars were bought for the fun of it. The Derby Bentley, the vee-twelve Lagonda, the Type-135 Delahaye and even the short chassis 850 series Horch reflect this trend ... The chauffeur-driven

limousine survived but now it was based on inexpensive and popular chassis – Humber and Vauxhall in England, F.I.A.T. in Italy and Renault in France.'

With the advent of mass production, and increased emphasis on comfort, designers now took over more and more from engineers as the people to decree the next development. Although this resulted in some hideously pretentious bodies with vulgar radiators, the interest in aerodynamics led to attempts at streamlining the body, giving some models an almost futuristic look. Sir Dennistoun Burney, the airship engineer, designed a 3-litre streamlined saloon in 1930 and its impressive performance – 80mph being obtainable from 80bhp, although the car weighed 2 tons – led to more experiments. 1934 saw the appearance in America of the Chrysler Airflow, in Czechoslovakia the 2.9-litre air-cooled Tatra and in England the 11 hp Singer Airstream.

Strangest of all in shape was Voisin's Aerodyne 6-cylinder. In France at this time, as Lord Montagu points out, 'cars were bigger, their styling aped Chrysler and General Motors, and the dead hand of the *conduite interieure avec malle* as Michael Sedgwick has termed it, descended upon the industry ... The *conduite interieure avec malle* rolled its way down the *routes nationales* of the 1930s at a stolid 80 kilometres an hour, acquiring independent front suspension and synchromesh as it went, plus some of Detroit's nastier stylistic influences.'

One notable exception was the Delage. Having

The Pierce-Arrow

Gil Spear

[Shopping with the Pierce-Arrow]

French conversation piece in the late 1920s.

triumphed in racing in the 1920s, this firm's next development was the D8, first of the line of touring Delages described by Ralph Stein as 'the car of the *jeunesse dorée* of the thirties, at least for those for whom a Type 57 Bugatti was just too mechanical'. Although hardly suited to twisting English roads, the Figoni-built model 8-cylinder attracted quite a following across the Channel: secure behind its magnificent long bonnet, a driver could feel tremendous power, and all for about £1,500. This was, perhaps, the Continent's most interesting car in the period leading up to the Second World War.

In Britain, for the man who could not afford a Rolls-Bentley there was snob value in owning a foreign car, and in the thirties French and American cars made increasing inroads on the British luxury market. What was depressing was the shape of most of the smaller cars which appeared as boxes on wheels. This led to a new phenomenon, the packager, who took a mass-produced chassis and designed for it a special body to suit its own adopted 'house' style. The outstanding example, one that challenged the traditional luxury car with conspicuous and lasting success, was the low-slung SS, later the SS Jaguar.

William Lyons furnished a 16hp standard chassis with 'a rakish coupé, with a very long bonnet, helmet-type cycle wings and a relatively deep windscreen, in spite of which the complete car stood a mere 4' 7″ off the ground'. By

1934 the SSI looked smart enough to attract those who had been taken aback by the first model, the additional power now enabling it to lap in a sports-car race at nearly 80mph. A year later it deserved, justly, to be named among the sleekest animals: it cost only £385 but looked well worth £1,000. William Lyons produced 5,378 cars in 1939: 'He had achieved marvels by producing and selling a genuine 100mph car – the 3½-litre SS. 100 – at £445.'

As war once again engulfed the world, we may look back with Leonard Woolf over the preceding two decades. He is on record as saying: 'Nothing ever changed so profoundly my material existence, the mechanism and range of my every-day life, as the possession of a motor car.'

But the real sign of those times was the spread from America into Europe of the mass market, with all that this would mean for people everywhere. Here, in car ownership, was the gate to freedom. In the 1930s the sea, the railway and the air were still, over the longer distances, the preserve of the few; only the road, it seemed, could lead the common man to his El Dorado.

And so it has, though gradually, as the juggernaut's influence engulfs us and rends the fabric of the older civilizations, we are all beginning to rue the cost. The designers and engineers of the 1920s and 1930s have indeed much to answer for.

7 ROAD TRAVEL: THE AMERICAN STORY

In the early 1920s, as the USA began to assert itself in the world, the nation's wealthiest citizens wanted cars that symbolized their success and power. Ten years later, however, when Wall Street had crashed, some of those rich who were still rich preferred, more cautiously, to hide their good fortune and drive unostentatious cars.

In that giddy first decade a breed of exotic, luxurious motor car was created in America, the names of which have passed into legend: Duesenberg, Stutz, Cord, Packard, Auburn, Pierce-Arrow. They were bigger, brasher, beefier than all but a few European marques, and their like will not be seen again.

America's prestige cars did not happen suddenly in a burst of opulence and innovation. From the first days of motoring the United States always had a few makers of sumptuous motors. Often, as in Europe, these firms were former carriage-builders adapting their bodies with varying successes to the dictates of the internal combustion engine.

The tradition of luxury motoring is rather strange considering the appalling state of American roads in the first quarter of the century, a state hardly conducive to the creation of thoroughbred cars. Even in 1919, according to *The Age of Motoring Adventure 1897-1939*, 'the big heavy touring car would roll along ... would meet a nasty patch and with broken dignity would heave and sigh from side to side as it slowly crawled in bottom gear over the ridges and furrows ... One could hear every joint groan under the strain and could sometimes see the bottom of the engine scrape ridges into the chunks of earth ...' And even worse for the humbler motor cyclist: 'When I say that there is no other road for a hundred miles to the south and unspeakable miles to the north, you will know what I mean. Repeatedly ... I had to get out and skirmish around to find traces of the road at all.' It seems, nevertheless, that 'the Americans think they are great road-builders ... Yet ninety-five per cent or more of America's highways are dirt roads, or what they are pleased to call "Natural Gravel". In many cases they comprise merely a much-worn trail and as often as not a pair of ruts worn in the prairie ... the roads and streets in the cities are bad ... I have seen places in Broadway where the tram-lines wander six or seven inches above the surface of the road.' Fortunately, improvement of American roads was to be both rapid and immense. By 1927 there were already three miles of paved road to one of railroad, and by 1939 the highway network of the United States was regarded as the best in the world.

One of the earliest prestige cars was the Locomobile of Bridgeport, Connecticut. This firm started off in 1899 with a version of the Stanley Steamer, and by 1918 was producing cars with T-head 90hp petrol engines. It boasted: 'No stock parts or ready made units are permitted.'

Not surprisingly, Locomobiles were extremely expensive, costing $4,800 in 1912 and $9,600 in 1929, when the company finally collapsed. As he recalls in his *Autobiography*, Charles Chaplin set out in 1916 to buy his first car. His earnings, already 'legendary', were to him only 'a

DE SOTO SIX

PRODUCT of CHRYSLER

Sedan de Lujo, $955 at Factory
Special equipment extra

$845

and up, at the factory

MODISH, BEAUTIFUL — and FINE THROUGHOUT

De Soto Six, despite its most moderate price, has been singled out as a fashionable car. It is fit companion for the larger, costlier cars in the most exacting homes. It rides with a richness of ease unknown in its class. It is not merely amply powered but magnificently so, and it is fine throughout. In the De Soto Six, at last high quality and moderate price are joined together.

Visit De Soto Six exhibits at Chicago Automobile Show and Congress Hotel, January 26-February 2.

DE SOTO MOTOR CORPORATION (*Division of Chrysler Corporation*), *Detroit, Michigan*

symbol in figures, for I had never actually seen it. I therefore had to do something to prove that I had it. So I procured a secretary, a valet, a car and a chauffeur. Walking by a show room one day, I noticed a seven-passenger Locomobile, which, in those days, was considered the best car in America. The thing looked too magnificently elegant to be for sale. However I walked into the shop and asked: "How much?" "Four thousand nine hundred dollars." "Wrap it up," I said.

'The man was astonished and tried to put up a resistance to such an immediate sale. "Would you like to see the engine?" he asked. "Wouldn't make any difference – I know nothing about them," I answered. However I pressed the tyre with my thumb to show a professional touch.'

Locomobile was unusual for luxury builders because it produced the whole car and did not allow other custom houses to make bodies for Locomobile chassis. The Franklin company from Syracuse, New York, however, preferred its clients to get a body from elsewhere to go with its car's chassis and 6-cylinder air-cooled engine. Franklins were generally bodied by the Derham, Willoughby,

Holbrook or Dietrich firms. Colonel Charles Lindbergh was particularly fond of Dietrich Franklins and his fellow flier, Ameria Earhart, was also a customer.

In 1930, a Dietrich-bodied speedster with the same engine that was used in the Waco biplane was selling for $7,200. In 1932 Franklin unveiled its Series 17 supercharged V12s which produced 150hp but only reached 95mph flat out. The reason for this was perhaps that the solid chassis and luxurious Dietrich body weighed over three tons. There were few buyers, especially at $4,400. A year later the company slashed the price to $2,885 but to no avail. In 1934, after thirty-three years in the car business, Franklin cut its losses and pulled out, turning the plant over to aero-engine production.

Another company, Peerless, from Cleveland, Ohio, staggered through the Depression and in 1931 gave up carmaking for beer production. Before the First World War this firm had been known as 'one of the three Ps', the others being Pierce-Arrow and Packard. The Peerless reputation was, however, based on product reliability rather than body design, the latter often being rather uninspired. But in 1930 the marque flowered brilliantly for one magnificent

year when the designs of the prolific Count Alexis de Sakhnoffsky led to the production of beautiful cars with straight-six and -eight engines, selling for between $995 and $2,195.

The Cunningham company of Rochester, New York, started life in 1909. In 1921 it produced a good-looking, mechanically conventional V8 100hp car, with a few body options. At $9,000 each, it would have taken a Marshall Field, William Randolph Hearst, Mary Pickford or Harold Lloyd to afford one – and, as it happens, they all did. This firm's attraction was its consummate craftsmanship: it built slowly and surely. It is not altogether surprising that in 1933, when the luxury market was in decline, Cunningham switched to building hearses, with the occasional ambulance produced as a rush order.

Pierce-Arrow of Buffalo, New York, stayed the course a little longer. They began producing quality motors in 1901 and only collapsed in 1938, long after most of the great names had disappeared. The Pierce-Arrows, with much of the exclusiveness of a Rolls-Royce, embodied fussy, almost snooty touches. Except in 1928, the Pierce-Arrow name never appeared on a radiator: the cars were supposed to be

recognizable without it. And it was not until 1920 that, with evident regret at the barbarian course they felt obliged to follow, the Pierce-Arrow directors consented to produce their cars with steering wheels on the left.

The earlier Pierce-Arrow style was massive and luxurious. In 1914, there was a 6-cylinder model, with a 12ft 3in wheelbase and 37in wheels. This car was supplied with two bodies, one open, one closed, the change-over being easily made by the chauffeur with the aid of a few strong men. In 1920 Fatty Arbuckle took delivery of a custom-built Pierce-Arrow of particular vastness but, by 1923, it was evident that these cars were rather too large. A smaller Model 80 was introduced but it was only a modest success and, in 1928, the company was taken over by Studebaker.

The name lived on. At the 1933 Century of Progress Exhibition in Chicago, the exquisite Pierce-Arrow Silver Arrow was one of the show stoppers; only five of these cars were ever built. They had a 12-cylinder 175hp engine, power brakes, airline styling and cost $10,000 each. But it was to be a brief burst of glory. In 1935 Pierce-Arrow was sold again, this time to a group of Buffalo businessmen:

they tried to restore flagging sales by racing and speed-record attempts but, within three years, the company was finished.

The McFarlan name stood for perspicacity and cars of the same high order as Cunningham. In its best year this fastidious company from Connersville, Indiana, managed to produce only 235 cars. Established in 1910, the firm always used straight-six or -eight engines and offered a wide range of body options. In 1920, it introduced its TV series of large cars using a twin-valve 6-cylinder engine with triple ignition and no less than eighteen spark plugs. Such an ornate engine was well-suited to McFarlan's over-elaborate town car, the so-called Knickerbocker Cabriolet, which was on offer in 1921 for $9,000. The company's select band of customers eventually dwindled, however, and from 1923 to 1928 McFarlan tried abortively to produce cheaper cars. The firm met a sad but important end in 1928 when it was bought by Erret Cord.

Erret Labbon Cord was a businessman whose greatest skill was in organizing talent. Two years before buying out Franklin, the Indianapolis-based entrepreneur had merged his Auburn-Cord company with a six-year old firm, the name of which was to become legend. That name was Duesenberg, but, unlike most myths, the closer we look at the story of Duesenberg the larger it becomes.

Fred Duesenberg unveiled his first car, the Model A, in 1920. With high-class engineering as his forte he pioneered four-wheel hydraulic brakes, working 16in forged drums to halt the momentum created by the modest (by later standards) 90hp engine. The asking price was a prestigious $6,500 but the car was not an immediate success, few people knowing the Duesenberg name.

Such obscurity could not last long. In April 1920 Tommy Milton growled up to the start of a measured mile in a 16-cylinder Duesy Special. Just 23.07 seconds later the Duesenberg had snatched the world record from Packard, with a speed of 156.04mph. Then, with little more ado, Duesenberg won the French Grand Prix, the Indianapolis 500 *and* world acclaim.

Now advertisements for Duesenberg could read: 'The world's champion automobile, built to outclass, outrun and outlast any car on the road' or, more poetically: 'Volume is not in his (Fred Duesenberg's) line of things. He is an engineer with a touch of devotion to his work like a Beethoven or a Rembrandt ... A Duesenberg is a thing of fineness and precision – a stress-enduring, masterful mechanical creation – a veritable symphony in steel.'

When the Duesenbergs triumphed at Indianapolis it was a victory won in the factory's own back garden. At this time few manufacturers had their own test tracks, and Duesenberg took full advantage of the Indianapolis circuit just $2\frac{1}{2}$ miles from his shops. One spectacular proving stunt

Jack Dempsey, the world heavyweight champion, in the cockpit of his immaculate Chrysler Imperial, poses for the camera with an approving crowd of onlookers in 1930.

Z-35-

was a non-stop three-month drive at a steady 40mph which, to a languidly stroking Duesenberg engine, was easy going. Unfortunately, the trial went wrong when a senior company employee visited the track with his over-eager son, who took over the driving. The Duesenberg was raced up to 100mph, at which point a rod broke. It took the furious engineers two hours to make good before the run continued, without further mishap.

Another test with the early straight-eight engine was a circuit of 3,155 miles around the Indianapolis track in just over two days, at an average speed of 62.63mph. Planned so that the car need not stop, driver change-overs and refuelling were done from another Duesenberg that came alongside and locked in with a special bumper. Unfortunately, the run was twice interrupted by punctures.

Duesenberg's merger with Auburn-Cord cleared the way for the next creation. It took two years to finalize but, in 1928, there emerged the first of the classic Duesenbergs, a huge beast of unheard-of proportions. The 1928 J Duesenberg had a 7-litre straight-eight engine giving out no less than 265hp, twice the power of any other American car. At a time when 90mph in top gear was considered fantastic, the J Duesenberg topped 90mph in *second*; and anyone who had the nerve to pull it into top could touch 116mph.

This mighty engine was as delicately balanced as the working of Big Ben. Maximum power came at only 4,200 revs, which perhaps explains why fifty years later so many of these muscle-bound engines still run sweetly. Duesenberg supplied no bodies, but with his chassis, kept rigid by six cross members, came among other refinements a dashboard with a tachometer, a stop-watch chronometer, a brake pressure gauge and an altimeter barometer.

There were also four warning lights. One blinked every 750 miles to remind the driver to change his oil; another every 1,500 miles to tell him to top up the battery; and a third to advise replenishment of the automatic chassis lubrication system. By 1930 a Duesenberg chassis cost an incredible $14,000 and, with bodywork of suitable distinction, the bill would give little change from $25,000. And the coachbuilders who graced this huge chassis were the aristocrats of their craft: Murphy, Bohman and Schwartz, Judkins, Derham, LeBaron, Millspaugh and Irish, Springfield and Rubay, Bender, McNeer, Union City, Fleetwood, Shutte and McFarland.

The Duesenberg was undoubtedly the most spectacular car of its age and it attracted some of the most spectacular buyers. The kings of Spain and Italy ordered them, Queen Marie of Yugoslavia used one and Prince Nicholas of Rumania owned two. In the United States, Mayor Jimmy Walker of New York was very proud of his Duesy and Mae West is supposed to have said that she would not be seen dead without one. The big beasts also matched the tastes and pockets of celebrities like William Randolph Hearst, Tommy Manville, Elizabeth Arden, Gary Cooper and Clark Gable. And in 1932 came the ultimate Duesenberg, the SJ: supercharging the already mighty J engine gave this

monster no less than 320hp and a top speed of 130 mph.

Fred Duesenberg was killed in one of the new SJs in 1932. A year later the company displayed its last extravagance at the Century of Progress Exhibition with the Twenty Grand Rollsten sedan on an SJ chassis, so-called because the car cost, literally, $20,000. Cord continued production of these king cars until 1937. There were to be no more sensational developments, but enough had already been achieved to create the undying legend.

Fashions in motor cars, as in much else, were set by Hollywood's film stars. Here is a stylish favourite of Clark Gable, combining size, speed and opulence.

The second string of the Cord bow was the Auburn range, generally neat, distinctive and inexpensive cars. In 1931 Cord marketed a 160hp Auburn V12 Speedster which sold for less than $1,000. The Speedster, partly because of its transverse golf-bag locker and a facia plaque testifying it had exceeded 100mph, was a favourite with film stars who had not quite moved into the big league.

Cord's third great marque bore his own name. The first Cord, the L29, was produced in 1929 around a straight-eight engine but at $3,000 it was too expensive for what it was. It sold modestly and, in 1932, Cord scrapped it. But three years later his designer Gordon Buehrig, a member of the Auburn Speedster team, produced perhaps the greatest jolt that car design has ever received. While the 1934

Chrysler Airflow may have been a consummate exercise in overcoming wind resistance, it was extremely ugly. The 1935 Model 810 Cord, on the other hand, was extremely attractive.

Started originally as a smaller Duesenberg, it had been the victim of many changes yet what emerged was a most striking car with front-wheel drive from a V8 and such features as retractable headlights, hidden door-hinges and that famous door-to-door radiator grille. With its clean smooth lines and unfussy exterior, this car spelt final doom to the old 'sit-up-and-beg' designs.

E L Cord abandoned car building in 1937. The Duesenberg, Auburn and Cord were finished. It was the end of an era. For Cord's empire, like many others, had no

fat to tide it over lean times: even in the palmy 1920s it was never that easy to sell the more expensive cars.

Yet one remarkable company, able evidently to sell prestige cars like Henry Ford sold Model Ts, survived the bad years, outliving most of its rivals. The first great Packard was the 7-litre V12 of 1916, the Twin Six. This remained in production until 1923 and established a solid reputation that led to buyers such as President Warren G Harding, King Alexander of Yugoslavia and Tsar Nicholas II. Whatever their politics, Russians seemed to prefer Packards: like the Tsar before him, Joseph Stalin bought one, this being the 1927 Super Eight model.

In 1928, despite the difficult times and the price of $4,000, Packard sold an incredible fifty thousand straight-eights. By 1930 it was estimated that this phenomenal company was selling half of all the luxury cars in the world.

Packard was a strange company. On the one hand it resolutely refused to undertake the type of annual styling changes with which mass producers had been burdening the industry while, on the other, it could be amazingly flamboyant. When it produced a sporty runabout, a plaque was screwed to the facia of each one guaranteeing that the vehicle had been driven 250 miles by the American racing ace Tommy Milton. Luckily for Milton, only 150 of these were sold but, even so, he had to drive nearly 40,000 miles for this unusual exercise.

In 1927 Packard invested $1 million in its own custom-built testing ground and became the first motor manufacturer to boast one. The grounds at Utica, Michigan, 21 miles from the Detroit factory provided garaging for a score of vehicles, $2\frac{1}{2}$ miles of banked concrete speedway, and 12 miles of rough roads with artificial inclines, rivers, sand pits and paving. The company used this motoring torture chamber both for development projects and for proving random samples off the production line. At the end of its test, each vehicle was taken to pieces and examined minutely to see how every part had taken the strain.

In 1930 Packard introduced the Model 734 Speedster

which, unusually for American cars, had four forward gears (instead of three) to govern its power. This car, capable of 100mph, is now a collector's item, since production lasted for only a year. Then came the Packard 12 Sports Sedan, presented as the 'Car of the Dome' at the 1933 Chicago exhibition, with a price tag of $12,000.

Packards were now successfully combining mechanical excellence, reliability and fresh styling. Differing wheel bases offered scope to body-builders, among them Le-Baron who produced three beautiful sports coupés in 1934 at $18,000 each. In 1937, the year the mighty Duesenberg breathed its last, Packard, the great survivor, sold an amazing 109,518 units.

Chicago gangsters were among those who liked Packards but the mobs also had a taste for Packard's main and most effective rival, Cadillac. This firm started in 1903 making single-cylinder cars, a modesty for which they atoned later with monstrous 16-cylinder engines. But their fame rested on a V8 engine introduced in 1914 which became a byword for unrelenting efficiency.

Cadillac engines became progressively mightier in the search for fast, quiet motoring. In 1931 they introduced a V12 and in 1937 the V16. The latter offered 185hp from a $7\frac{1}{2}$-litre capacity, a weight above three tons and a thirst at the rate of a gallon of fuel every four miles. In its advertisements, Cadillac called its products 'The Standard of the World'. Sales were global and came close to matching Packard's.

With a Cadillac went style with a dash of panache. Tom Laughton recalls in *Pavilion by the Sea* how he went to stay in the 1930s with Leonard Hannah at his Cleveland mansion. 'On my first morning I was awakened by an elderly English butler who, as he drew the curtains, enquired: "What time would you like the car, sir." "I haven't got a car," I replied. "The car that Mr. Leonard has provided for you," was his dignified rejoinder. It seemed too much, so I didn't order it.

'Downstairs at breakfast Leonard said to me: "I hear

Two film personalities of the 1930s, Jean Harlow (left) and Gary Cooper, pose carefully with their cars of the moment in settings which, appropriately, denote high society, wealth and influence.

MARLENE DIETRICH
in Paramount

you won't use the car." I told him that he was too generous. He replied "I have a Cadillac and a chauffeur for the use of my guests, you are the first guest I have had in the last three months; if you won't use the car the chauffeur will probably commit suicide." So, for the rest of my visit, I was rolling around Cleveland in a chauffeur-driven Cadillac.'

According to David Niven in *The Moon's a Balloon*, Marlene Dietrich's Cadillac also could hardly be ignored. 'The premières of the big pictures were black tie events and all the big names turned out to cheer on their friends. Outside, "bleachers" were erected to enable the screaming fans to catch a glimpse of their favourites and searchlights waved weaved patterns across the sky. After the show, a loudspeaker alerted the fans to the departing of the great.

Above: The ever-lovely Marlene Dietrich in informal attire allows herself to be paired with, but not outshone by, this sleek, black monster of a rich person's truly de luxe automobile.

'Modern as Tomorrow': a hard-selling 1939 American magazine advertisement, aimed at luxury-loving but price-conscious lady drivers, of the sleek, opulent Dodge 'Luxury Liner' limousine.

MODERN AS TOMORROW

Miss Mabel Ellis Asks:

"Can I Get A Big Car That's *Easy* On Gas And Oil?"

Miss Mabel Ellis,
New York, N. Y.

Go to Your Dodge Dealer, Miss Ellis

TAKE A LOOK

...That's all DODGE asks!

TAKE A LOOK! New Individual-Action Front Wheel Springing, with Amola Steel springs, gives new driving sureness!

TAKE A LOOK! New kind of speedometer — with a "safety light" on speed indicator that glows green up to 30 miles per hour; amber from 30 to 50; red beyond 50!

TAKE A LOOK! Famous Dodge "Scotch Dynamite" Engine—with all the proven Dodge economy features, plus new advances for even more efficient operation!

LIKE Miss Ellis, thousands of new car buyers are asking: "What 1939 car offers big-car luxury at small first cost, and low operating economy as well?"

An important question, of course. So important that Dodge thinks you should learn the answer first-hand. So we simply say: "Go to your Dodge dealer and see what Dodge has to offer. Be critical. Test Dodge against others. Then decide for yourself!"

In other words, "Take a Look... that's all Dodge asks!" Take a look at Dodge's new beauty, greater roominess, and wealth of new ideas —more than have ever been built into any new Dodge model!

By all means, take a look at the famous Dodge "Scotch Dynamite" Engine. It's greater than ever this year—offers new advancements for even more efficient operation! Add to this Dodge's world-famous Dependability—it means even greater savings in long life and trouble-free service.

Then take a look at the price tag! With all its extra value, this big Luxury Liner sells for *even less* than last year's Dodge!

Tune in on Major Bowes, Columbia Network, Thursdays, 9:00 to 10:00 P. M. E. D. S. T.

Dodge Coupes, $756 and up; Sedans, $815 and up, delivered in Detroit, including all standard equipment and all Federal Taxes. Transportation, state and local taxes (if any), extra.

The New 1939 DODGE Luxury Liner

Mr. Clark Gable's car! Miss Marlene Dietrich's car! Miss Constance Bennett's car! Miss Shirley Temple's mother's car! and on one glorious occasion – Mr. Alfred Hitchcar's cock!

'Marlene Dietrich had a black Cadillac driven by a chauffeur named Briggs who carried two revolvers and in winter wore a uniform with mink collar.'

The man who founded Cadillac in 1903, Henry M Leland, resigned in 1917 to start the Lincoln company. His first car, a five-passenger tourer, came on the market in 1921. It had a V8 engine, just like a Cadillac, and sold for $4,600. Leland's next marque was not as successful and, in 1922, Lincoln went bankrupt. But Henry Ford who had long wanted to make cars for the rich (as well as for everyone else) bought the Lincoln shell for a very generous $8 million.

As a prince of industry, Ford was perhaps better placed than many manufacturers to ensure that his cars fell into the right hands. In 1924, President Coolidge bought a Lincoln, so starting the White House's Lincoln tradition. This survived, rather as Daimlers were for long the favourite car of the British Royal Family. Although the Lincolns undoubtedly belonged at the top of the market, Ford soon sought the best of both worlds. Edsel Ford's inspiration, the Lincoln Zephyr, incorporating Chrysler's new airflow lines, was supposedly the first V12 priced for the average American. But the car, in truth an up-rated Ford V8, was not a success.

Even so, Lincoln finished the 1930s on a much more promising note. The first Lincoln Continental was created in 1939 by designers with Edsel Ford looking over their shoulders. The convertible which Ford had made especially for himself included such new luxuries as hydraulic windows and seat adjustment, flashing signals and, luxury of luxuries, a pedal for tuning the radio.

Buick, a substantial, essentially 'middle-class' product, like the British Rover, made some excursions into the world of luxury. The marque was popular in Britain where one DA series straight-eight drove into history when it carried Mrs Wallis Simpson into exile where Edward VIII was soon to join her.

Also popular in Britain was the car which, after Duesenberg, had perhaps the most glamorous name in the American galaxy of motoring giants: the Stutz. Harry C Stutz started his company in 1913 in Indianapolis with a car called Bearcat. But ten years later so little had happened to advance the Stutz fortunes that the firm was taken over by Charles M Swab. Under the new owner the company took on some potent design talent, including Paul Bastein from the prestigious Belgian Metallurgique firm, and Frederick E Moskovics, who had been with Marmon. In 1926 the company produced the Stutz AA. Sold as 'The Safety Car', a year's free insurance was supplied with it.

Stutz stayed with straight-eight engines until the company folded in 1935. What Stutz lacked in flair was made up with rakish, aggressive styles. In 1927 Moskovics unveiled the Black Hawk: like the later Packard Model 734,

this was a four-gear car, with a speedster option, pulled by a bored-out engine.

In 1928, Stutz entered racing to prove the cars and bolster their reputation. A supercharged Stutz Black Hawk Speedster promptly won the Atlantic City 150-mile race at an average speed of 96.3mph. Close on its tail were two more Stutzes. That year, too, a Stutz came second at Le Mans, almost beating a Bentley.

But this was also the year when Moskovics lost a $25,000 bet when a Black Hawk was beaten in a well-publicized 24-hour challenge race against a Hispano-Suiza at

Indianapolis. The humiliation was not dissipated when another Black Hawk beat a Hispano by 7 miles in a 3½-hour rematch: the news of the first Stutz defeat had been reported too well. The final misfortune for Stutz came when Frank Lockhart tried for the Landspeed record at Daytona in a Black Hawk. The car crashed and Lockhart, a brilliant young driver, was thrown out and killed.

The last offering was the splendid Stutz, an ultra-luxurious car designed by Roberts of the LeBaron firm. It had only a limited success and the company sank towards closure. In 1935 it stopped producing cars and began instead to make light delivery vans known as 'Pak-Age Cars': a miserable end.

Among the other notable smaller companies which disappeared in the 1930s were Marmon, Du Pont and Brewster. Based originally on Long Island, New York, Brewster moved in 1934 to Springfield, Massachusetts. As befitted a firm which began life making carriages, Brewster's main talent was body-building. It was its link with and, later, absorption by a distinguished Springfield neighbour, Rolls-Royce, which prevented Brewster's premature disappearance.

Another film star, Paramount's Kitty Carlisle, in immaculate juxtaposition with, undoubtedly, the right car in the right place.

At the end of the First World War Rolls-Royce was irked by the high import duties keeping its United States sales depressed. For a firm as cautious as Rolls, its solution was quite adventurous: it decided to make an 'American' Rolls. In November 1919 it bought a plant in Springfield and began tooling up with dies and parts sent from England. Two years later the company produced its first cars known as Silver Ghosts. In 1926, after expensive retooling, it changed over to producing the Phantom I.

Unfortunately, however, the ultimate British status symbol failed at that time to win favour in the United States, despite such advertisements as: 'There is a woman so fastidious she has been known to spend hours dressing for a ball ... so artistic she has furnished her house with rich treasures from the ends of the earth ... so sagacious she handles her own considerable financial affairs. She drives, or is driven in, a Rolls-Royce on every motoring occasion. Only this best car, from every point of view, could please a nature so many-sided, so discriminating as hers.'

The Depression finished the American branch of this company in 1931. Less than three thousand cars had been sold, many of them bodied by the painstaking Brewster concern. Was this failure the price to be paid for what someone unkindly called 'the triumph of craftsmanship over design', or was it only to be expected as the self-effacing patter of the British-trained salesman became drowned by the brasher, more exotic roar of the Duesenbergs? More likely, the demise of *all* those great, handsome and splendidly idiosyncratic cars was just one of the early signs of times which, since, have seen an end to the 'grand' days of travel. The first hints of the slowly rising tide of mediocre uniformity were already evident by the end of the 1920s. Here is one of them from Charles Black's *Motorists' Reference and Year Book for 1928*: 'Motoring in America has reached the stage where it is regarded by the mass of the public in that country purely as an essential means of transport. The average American of today has little time or interest for the mechanical detail and what we know as refinement of performance; he takes the minimum possible interest in maintenance and the act of driving. He insists upon a car that will "get him there" without making any demand upon his intelligence, time or skill.' Then, 'High speeds on the American roads are seldom possible ... At really high speeds American cars are inclined to bounce.'

Today, alas, not even the bounce survives.

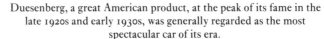

Duesenberg, a great American product, at the peak of its fame in the
late 1920s and early 1930s, was generally regarded as the most
spectacular car of its era.

ENGLISH-AMERICAN GLOSSARY

accumulator	battery
bonnet	hood
boot	trunk
bottom gear	low gear
capacity (engine)	displacement
carburettor	carburetor
change gear	shift gear
dickey	rumble seat
estate car	station wagon
gear lever	shift lever
hood (folding)	top
indicator	turn signal
lamps	lights
lorry	truck
motor car	automobile
mudguard	fender
petrol	gasoline
saloon	sedan
shooting brake	station wagon
silencer	muffler
spanner	wrench
starting handle	crank handle
top gear	high gear
tyre	tire
wind	crank
windscreen	windshield
wing	fender

(With acknowledgement to Lord Montagu of Beaulieu and
F Wilson McComb in *Behind the Wheel*)

le Lujo, $955 at Factory
cial equipment extra

Distinguished guests arrive by
car for a 1929 Hollywood film
première: as David Niven relates,
a black tie event with all the big
names there to cheer their
friends.

Cunard's *Caronia*, a recent favourite with cruising Americans, seen here against New York's brilliant skyline, often a European's awe-inspiring first glimpse of the New World.

Expectations of travel and of new ways of getting about the world were generally lower in 1945, in the new atomic age at the end of the Second World War, than they had been in the optimistic, idealistic days following the First World War. Most countries were now bent on picking up their pre-war pieces, on getting back to 'normal'. Only in the United States of America, which had emerged as the richest, strongest and most zestful nation on earth, did the immediate future seem full of promise and achievement.

Even in that country, however, apart from the development of regular non-stop transatlantic air services using land planes, there was little that could be called new in the realm of public transportation. Thus old friends, great survivors among the momentarily half-forgotten ocean liners, shorn of their dull war-paint, reappeared in their owners' fineries and, soon, were plying the famous mail routes of the world as though nothing much had happened since their early, halcyon débuts. For a long time to come the bulk of passenger traffic between North America and the Old World would be concentrated, once again, on the shipping routes connecting New York with North-west Europe. The life-style of liner passengers, although less ostentatious, the age of the common man being imminent, was essentially unchanged: there were the same lavish facilities, the same flunkey-type service, gargantuan meals and, in first class, evening dress for dinner, tombola and the dancing.

How long could it last? According to Douglas Phillips-Birt: 'In 1957, more passengers crossed the Atlantic by sea than ever before, and the profits of the lines were a comfort. The journal *Shipbuilding and Shipping Record* exclaimed in 1959: "The western world is becoming richer, not poorer, and there can be little doubt that the sumptuousness of future *Queens* will be as much in demand as now".'

But, despite the growing threat of jet travel, the signs were not being well read. 'The last of the old-style North Atlantic luxury liners, the *France*, went into service in 1961' and eight years later 'came the *Queen Elizabeth 2*, born of many doubts and false starts ... She is, Jack Newcombe has written, "a ship boldly conceived by the *Economist* Intelligence Unit, admirably design co-ordinated by Dennis Lennon, efficiently computerised from engine-room to bakery by Ferranti Argos and impeccably navigated by space satellite".

'There is nothing of the Ritz hotels in the *QE2*. She has the appeal of the best hotel in a seaside resort, one that retains the smartness of being a little less than popularly over-run, though with more emphasis on appeal to youth than such hotels usually offer.' The arguments about how many classes to provide were decided eventually 'in favour of a ship carrying only two classes and capable of sailing as a single-class ship. Compared with the *Queen Elizabeth*, the gross tonnage of the *QE2* is 65,000 as against 83,600, but she carries almost the same number of passengers, has one more deck and three-quarters of the crew. So luxury for the few is replaced by comfort and fun for the many.'

The liners lingered on. In the late summer of 1970 there were yet twelve sailings a month from New York to Western European ports, with passages on offer during August/September in *QE2*, *France*, *Bremen*, *Europa*, *Rotterdam*, *Nieuw Amsterdam*, *Statendam*, *Raffaello*, *Michelangelo*, *Cristoforo Colombo* and *Leonardo da Vinci*.

And now? While some of these fine ships, joined by newcomers of equal or greater luxury purpose-built for tourists, are engaged in pleasure cruising, Cunard's *QE2* alone survives as a true transatlantic liner, with regular sailings in the summer months between New York, Southampton and Cherbourg. And with much the same story from all the other once-busy shipping routes the world over, the glory has, for sure, departed.

In amenity and ambience, however, there is one form of travel today that bears some resemblance to the interwar variety, and that is travel by rail. Although standardization has lowered levels in most parts of the world, there remains a handful of de luxe trains in the old tradition. Among the most spectacular are Australia's *Indian-Pacific* and South Africa's *Blue Train*. The former, which covers the 2,500 miles between Sydney and Perth in a little over $2\frac{1}{2}$ days, is an air-conditioned train, described in the *Thomas Cook International Timetable* as an 'All-sleeping car train with single-birth Roomettes, two-berth Twinettes, De luxe Suite and Lounge Car in first class, two-berth Twinettes and Cafeteria Club Car in economy class', with ordinary first- and second-class day cars and a refreshment car on some days between Sydney and Peterborough. Furthermore, a 'Motorail service (carriage of passengers' motor cars) is available between Port Pirie and Perth and vv'.

South Africa's *Blue Train*, also fully air-conditioned, runs between Cape Town and Pretoria through Johannesburg and caters solely for first-class passengers, covering the 1,000 miles in just over twenty-four hours. This sixteen-coach train, effectively a five-star hotel on wheels, offers every conceivable aid to sybaritic living. The accommodation includes a three-room suite with private bathroom, alcove bar, refrigerator, telephone and a table which, one way up, is a card table. All passengers are greeted by porters who insist on carrying every item of baggage and by the train manager who ensures that any whim, including instant service of drinks, will be satisfied. Wide, doorless, carpeted corridors connect the cars. Lavish fittings, a low ceiling and concealed lighting give the dining car the air and mood of a high-class restaurant.

As the price of the ticket, ranging from about £60 to £90 a head, covers all meals en route, there is every incentive to make the most of the appetizing menus, including full-scale English breakfasts. In the lounge car a white-jacketed bar-tender dispenses cocktails and every other kind of drink with *canapés* served on a silver tray. There is, of course, room service, even the morning newspaper being delivered with the tactful awakening call. This exceptional train is fully booked months in advance: and no wonder!

In Europe the *Orient Express*, in common with many of the former long-distance services, is no more, though the *Tauern-Orient* still provides through sleeping-cars between Munich and Athens; and there survives a through

The modern car ferry linking the growing network of motorways is a potent factor in the worldwide spread of man's lethal, oppressive, ubiquitous private chariot, the motor car.

Today, Europe can boast its fine, new species of fast, first-class only daytime Trans-Europ Expresses (right) with schedules to suit the businessman. The main growth in overnight rail travel, however, has been the car-sleeper express (below), catering mainly for the holiday-maker.

Rolls-Royce (opposite page), super car of the century, synonym for quality, timeless symbol of luxury and so, perhaps, the most appropriate epitaph for a book about The Grand Days of Travel.

sleeping-car, connecting with a train-steamer service from London, from Hook of Holland through Berlin to Moscow. Some overnight journeys are much improved: there is today the Paris–Rome *Palatino* and Paris–Madrid *Puerta del Sol*, somewhat outshining the *Rome Express* and *Sud Express* respectively, the *Puerta* having the advantage of adjustable wheels so that its sleeping cars can manage the differing French and Spanish gauges. The *Palatino* leaves the Gare du Lyon at about 19.30 hours and the *Puerta del Sol* Austerlitz at 18.00 hours, each train reaching its destination around 09.00 hours next morning; and there are, of course, refreshment cars on both trains.

But the main growth in overnight rail travel has been in the form of car-sleeper expresses: these, catering mainly for the holiday-maker, are for the most part a summer-time phenomenon, with only a few services operating the year round. By day, Europe can boast its fine, new species of Trans-Europ Expresses (TEEs). These are fast, first-class only, air-conditioned trains connecting several of the main cities of continental Europe. Their schedules are designed to suit the businessman and provide an alternative to air travel, the distances chosen being mostly favourable to the train on a city-centre to city-centre time-scale.

Among the TEEs are some of the long-established names, of which the *Rheingold* and the *Mistral* are perhaps the most glamorous of their modern kind. However, their very long runs make them untypical. Today's *Rheingold* provides through cars from Hook of Holland (connecting with the overnight packet from Harwich) to Geneva and Milan, and from Amsterdam to Geneva and Zurich. An instant connection with the *Rheinpfeil* at Duisburg provides a fast branch service through Frankfurt to Munich. Most sections of the train have full dining-car facilities; and the train offers arrival times at Geneva and Zurich in time for dinner and at Milan around 21.00 hours.

Speed still counts and more, perhaps, than other considerations, passenger traffic having been greatly boosted by the famous Japanese 'bullet' trains, the British high-speed trains, the fast-running French and German inter-city expresses and the stylish American Amtrack services. Trains may be less idiosyncratic, less exciting, less romantic than they were but the standard of comfort remains remarkably high; and the operators do, at least, try to get passengers where they aim to be safely, smoothly and in the shortest possible time.

In recent years the most sensational explosion in forms and volume of travel has, of course, been in the air and on the road. In the early 1960s, with the jet age already across our doorstep and the era of mass international tourism in the offing; with new motorways, car ferries, plentiful petrol and greater driving comfort, among other incentives, to lure the man in the street; and with the spread of affluence, the stage was set for today's global, swirling, nose-to-tail merry-go-round of ever-larger, ever-faster planes, and for the frantic, worldwide spread of man's lethal, oppressive, ubiquitous private chariot, the motorcar.

These widespread phenomena of the air and of the road, almost obliterating their forebears in volume, versatility and performance, are today all around us. They shrink the world. They rule the environment. They serve us while they dominate us. Welcome or not, beneficial or not, such universal stereotypes need no introduction here, have no place in a book about 'grand' days. For, by definition, our present epoch, the new age of the common man, is now with us and can offer small scope for the exceptional, for the high and mighty, for true splendour and magnificence.

The best that money can buy today is by and large the four-star standard: the Hilton, Sheraton, Holiday Inn, Grand Metropolitan and Trust House Forte atmosphere; the air-conditioned, piped-music, deep-frozen, smiling-hostess, service-included, expense-account ambience; the standardized, predictable décor and amenities of the wide-bodied jet, the airport terminal, the hired car, the motorway restaurant, the inter-city express, the executive office; the penthouse apartment, the massage parlour, the 'private' hospital and, ere long, no doubt, the charge-it-later four-star crematorium.

Be thankful for small mercies? Certainly. But pretend not otherwise: the *Grand Days of Travel* are, indeed, behind us.

SOURCES

Allen, Charles, (ed), *Plain Tales from the Raj: Images of British India in the Twentieth Century* (Andre Deutsch and BBC, London, 1975)

Arlen, Michael, *The Green Hat* (Collins, London, 1926)

Barron, James and Tubbs, D B, *Vintage Cars in Colour* (Batsford, London, 1960)

Behrman, S N, *Duveen* (Hamish Hamilton, London, 1953)

Bentley, W O, *The Autobiography of W O Bentley* (Hutchinson, London, 1961)

— —. *The Cars in my Life* (Hutchinson, London, 1961)

Bishop, George, *The Age of the Automobile* (Hamlyn, London, 1977)

Blight, Anthony, *Georges Roesch and the Invincible Talbot* (Grenville Publishing, London, 1970)

Bonsor, N R P, *North Atlantic Seaway* (T Stephenson, 1960)

Brinnin, John Malcolm, *The Sway of the Grand Saloon: A Social History of the North Atlantic* (Delacourte, USA, 1971, and Macmillan, London, 1972)

Buckley, J R, *Cars of the Connoisseur* (Batsford, London, 1960)

Cable, Boyd, *A Hundred Year History of the P & O Peninsular and Oriental Steam Navigation Company, 1837–1937* (Ivor Nicholson and Watson, London, 1937)

Cary, Alan L, *Mail Liners of the World* (Sampson Low, Marston, London, 1937)

Chandler, Raymond, *The Smell of Fear* (Hamish Hamilton, London, 1965)

Chaplin, Charles, *My Autobiography* (Bodley Head, London, 1964)

Clarke, Alan (ed), *The Private Papers of Viscount Lee of Fareham* (John Murray, London, 1974)

Cluett, Douglas (ed), with Learmouth, R and Nash, J, *The First Croydon Airport, 1915–1928* (Sutton Libraries and Arts Services, 1977)

Clutton, Cecil and Stanford, John, *The Vintage Motor Car* (Batsford, London, 1954)

Cobham, Alan, *Skyways* (Nisbett, London, 1925)

Dalton, Lawrence, *Those Elegant Rolls-Royce* (Dalton Watson, London, 1967)

Dewar McLintock, J, *Royal Motoring* (Foulis, London, 1962)

Dumont, Pierre, Barker, Ronald and Tubbs, Douglas B, *Automobiles and Automobiling* (Edita, Lausanne and Patrick Stephens, London, 1968)

Duval, G R, *British Flying Boats and Amphibians, 1909–1952* (Putnam, London, 1966)

Eells, George, *The Life That Late He Led* (W H Allen, London, 1967)

Emmons, Frederick, *Pacific Liners, 1927–72* (David & Charles, Newton Abbot, 1973)

Fitzgerald, F Scott, *The Last Tycoon* (Grey Walls, London, 1949)

Fleming, Peter, *Travels in Tartary* (Alden Press, Oxford, 1934)

Gann, Ernest K, *Fate is the Hunter* (Hodder & Stoughton, London, 1961)

Georgana, G N (ed), *Encyclopaedia of American Automobiles* (Ebury Press, London, 1968)

Gordon, Jan and Cora J, *On Wandering Wheels* (Bodley Head, London, 1929)

Grahame-White, Montague, *At the Wheel Ashore and Afloat* (Foulis, London, 1935)

Greene, Graham, *England Made Me* (Heinemann, London, 1935)

Hadfield, John (ed), *The Saturday Book 32* (Hutchinson, London, 1972)

Harrison, Rosina, *Rose: My Life in Service* (Cassell, London, 1975)

Higham, Charles, *Cecil B. de Mille* (W H Allen, London, 1974)

Higham, Robin, *Britain's Imperial Air Routes, 1918 to 1939* (Foulis, London, 1960)

Hoare, Sir Samuel, *India by Air* (Longmans Green, London, 1927)

Horner, Raymonde (a relation of the present author), personal recollections

Hough, Richard and Frostick, Michael, *A History of the World's Classic Cars* (Allen & Unwin, London, 1963)

Hudson, Kenneth, *Air Travel, A Social History* (Adams & Dart, Bath, 1972)

Huxley, Aldous, *Those Barren Leaves* (Chatto & Windus, London, 1925)

Jeffs, Group-Captain James (former Croydon air-traffic controller), personal recollections

Lacey, Robert, *The Queens of the North Atlantic* (Sigdwick & Jackson, London, 1973)

Laughton, Tom, *Pavilion by the Sea* (Chatto & Windus, London, 1971)

Lewis, Sinclair, *Dodsworth* (New York, 1929)

Lozier, Herbert, *The Car of Kings* (Chilton, Philadelphia, 1967)

McKenzie, W A, *Motormania* (Cassell, London, 1972)

Mannin, Ethel, *Young in the Twenties, A Chapter of Autobiography* (Hutchinson, London, 1971)

Marland, O P, (well-travelled business man), personal recollections

Masters, Brian, *The Dukes* (Blond Briggs, London, 1975)

Maugham, W Somerset, *Altogether* (William Heinemann, London, 1934)

Montagu of Beaulieu, Lord, *Jaguar* (Cassell, London, 1961)

— —. *Lost Causes of Motoring, Europe, Vols I and II* (Cassell, London, 1969 and 1971 respectively)

— —. and Georgano, G N, *Early Days on the Road* (Michael Joseph, London, 1974)

— —. and Wilson McComb, F, *Behind the Wheel* (Paddington Press, London, 1978)

Moorehead, Lucy (ed), *Freya Stark Letters, Vol 2: The Open Door, 1930-35* (Compton Russel, Wiltshire, 1975)

Morgan, Bryan (ed), *The Great Trains* (Patrick Stephens, Cambridge, and Edita, Lausanne, 1973). The present author contributed the chapter 'Great Trains of Europe'.

Murray, Marischal, *Union-Castle Chronicle, 1853–1953* (Longmans, Green, London, 1953)

Nicholson, T R (ed), *The Age of Motoring Adventure, 1897–1939* (Cassell, London, 1972)

Niven, David, *The Moon's a Balloon* (Hamish Hamilton, London, 1971)

Olley, Captain Gordon P, *A Million Miles in the Air* (Hodder & Stoughton, London, 1934)

Owen, Charles, *Independent Traveller* (Routledge & Kegan Paul, London, 1966)

— —. *Britons Abroad* (Routledge & Kegan Paul, London, 1968)

— —. *No More Heroes* (Allen & Unwin, London, 1975)

Page, Martin, *The Lost Pleasures of the Great Trains* (Weidenfeld & Nicolson, London, 1975)

Phillips-Birt, Douglas, *When Luxury Went to Sea* (David & Charles, Newton Abbot, 1971)

Post, Emily, *Etiquette* (Funk & Wagnalls, 1922, and Emily Post Institute, 1969)

Powell, Anthony, *From a View to a Death* (Heinemann, London, 1971)

Price, Paul, *Steam Trains* (Albany Books, London, 1978)

Pritchard, Anthony, *The Motor Racing Merchants* (Leslie Frewin, London, 1976)

Pudney, John, *The Seven Skies* (Putnam, London, 1959)

Purdy, Ken W, *Wonderful World of the Automobile* (MacGibbon & Kee, London, 1961)

Rae, John B, *American Automobile Manufacturers: The First Forty Years* (Chilton, New York, 1959)

Roberts, Peter, *A Picture History of the Automobile* (Ward Lock, London, 1973)

Rowe, Captain Basil L, *Under My Wings* (W H Allen, London, 1957)

Scott-Hill, Ian (recently retired from British Airways), personal recollections

Sedgwick, Michael, *Cars of the 1930s* (Batsford, London, 1970)

Stanford, Donald K, *Ile de France, A Biography* (Cassell, London, 1960)

Stein, Ralph, *The Automobile Book* (Hamlyn, London, 1961)

— —. The Great Cars (Hamlyn, London, 1967)

Swinson, Arthur, *The Great Air Race, England–Australia, 1934* (Cassell, London, 1968)

Taylor, W R and Munson, Kenneth, *History of Aviation* (New English Library, London, 1975)

van Doren Stern, Philip, *A Pictorial History of the American Automobile* (Viking Press, New York, 1953)

Vernon Gibbs, Commander (S) C R, Royal Navy, *Passenger Liners of the Western Ocean* (Staples, 1952)

Vuillet, Gérard, *Railway Reminiscences of Three Continents* (Nelson, London, 1968)

Wall, Robert, *Ocean Liners* (Collins, London, 1978)

Wilson, R M, *The Big Ships* (Cassell, London, 1956)

Winchester, Clarence (ed), *Railway Wonders of the World, Vols 1 and 2* (Amalgamated Press, London, 1936)

Woolf, Leonard *Downhill All the Way* (Hogarth Press, London, 1967)

Woon, Basil, *The Frantic Atlantic* (New York, 1927)

Yates, Dornford, *Jonah and Co* (Ward Lock, London, 1922)

Periodicals and other sources
Chapters 4 and 8
Geographical Magazine (London, December 1964)
Various issues of *Thomas Cook International Timetable (formerly Cook's Continental Timetable)*. Advice received from its present Editor, John Price, is gratefully acknowledged.

Chapter 5
Various issues of *Aeroplane* and *Flight* magazines (London, 1932) Publicity statements: *Imperial Airways Achievements* (London, 1938)

Chapters 6 and 7
Various issues of *Autocar, Sketch* and *Illustrated London News* magazines, London

The Motorist's Reference and Year Book (Charles Black, London, 1928)

Duesenberg Model A and Cord 810 and 812 (Profile Publications Nos 57 and 35 respectively)

ACKNOWLEDGEMENTS

The author acknowledges with heartfelt thanks the invaluable help with research from his wife, Felicity, his friend, Anthea Marland, and his fellow-scribe, Nigel Ash, the motoring writer, for Chapters 6, 5 and 7 respectively; and for the help with typing and organization of the paperwork from his tireless secretary, Kate Ashbrook.

PICTURE CREDITS

Autocar, 152; Chrysler Corporation, 189; Robert Estall, 200 top and bottom; Mary Evans Picture Library, 10, 11 centre and bottom, 14 bottom left, 58, 59, 61 bottom right, 112, 118, 119, 126 bottom, 127, 170, 171, 172; Fairchild Aerial Surveys Inc, 196–7; Fiat, 17 bottom right; Robert Harding Associates, 107, 161 right, 173, 177; *Illustrated London News*, 93 bottom; R. H. Kindig, Denver, Colorado, 108 top and bottom; Kobal Collection, 184–5, 186, 187, 188, 190–1, 194–5; The Mansell Collection, 74 top, 123, 146 top and bottom; Peter Newark's Historical Pictures, 13, 57 top, 164; Peter Newark's Western Americana, 9 top and bottom, 92, 105, 106, 110–11, 130 bottom right, 150, 179; Popperfoto, 7, 12–13, 14–15, 24–5, 28–9, 29 right, 30, 31, 32, 35 top and bottom, 36–7, 38 top and bottom, 39, 40–1, 41 top, 50, 64–5, 66–7, 67, 68, 70, 71, 82–3, 98–9, 101–1, 102, 129 top and bottom, 132, 145, 168–9, 174; C. Posthumus, 165, 166 top left; By kind permission of Mrs Pulley, 20 top and bottom, 21 top and bottom, 46 bottom, 47 top; Radio Times Hulton Picture Library, 16–17, 18–19, 22–3, 23 bottom right, 26, 27 top and bottom, 37 right, 42–3, 44–5, 46 top, 48–9, 54–5, 56, 60–1, 62–3, 69, 72, 73, 74 bottom, 75 top and bottom, 79, 80–1, 90–1, 91 right, 99 bottom right, 113, 124–5, 125 top right, 126 top, 142–3, 143 right, 146–7, 148–9, 154 top, 154–5, 156, 180, 181, 201; Railway Museum, York, 93 top; George Rainbird Ltd, 94–5, 144; Peter Roberts Collection, 182–3, 192; Ann Ronan Picture Library, 117; Spectrum Colour Library, 199; John Topham Picture Library, 11 top, 57 bottom, 76–7, 78, 83 right, 84, 87, 88 top and bottom, 89, 96 top left, 96–7, 114–15, 130–1, 133, 134–5, 135 top right, 136–7, 160–1, 162–3, 166–7.

Colour
Cooper-Bridgeman Library, 34 top; Mary Evans Picture Library, 34 bottom, 51 top and bottom, 52 top and bottom, 85 top and bottom, 86 top and bottom, 104, 139, 140 top and bottom, 157, 158, 176 bottom; Michael Holford Library/Octopus Books, 103 top and bottom, 122, bottom; New English Library, 121; Picturepoint Ltd, 176 top; Peter Roberts Collection, 33, 175; John Topham Picture Library, 122 top.